ROAD STORIES AND RECIPES

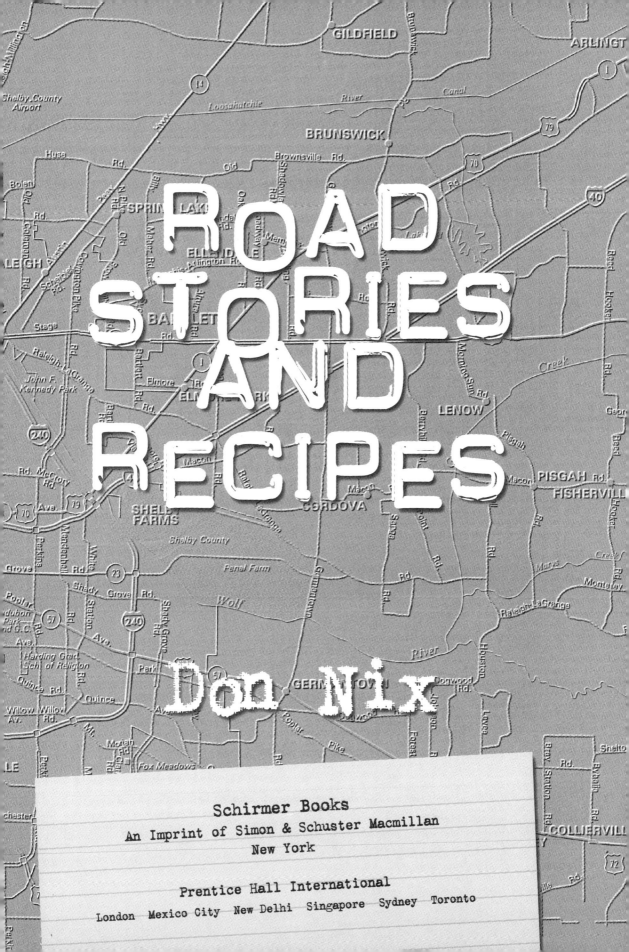

ROAD STORIES AND RECIPES

Don Nix

Schirmer Books

An Imprint of Simon & Schuster Macmillan

New York

Prentice Hall International

London Mexico City New Delhi Singapore Sydney Toronto

Schirmer Books
An Imprint of Simon & Schuster Macmillan
1633 Broadway
New York, NY 10019

Book Design: Rob Carangelo
© American Map Corporation

AmericanLibrary of Congress Catalog Card Number: 96-27474

Printed in the United States of America

Printing Number
1 2 3 4 5 6 7 8 9 10

Library of Congress Cataloging-in-Publication Data

Nix, Don, 1941–
    Road stories & recipes / Don Nix.
        p.   cm.
    Includes index.
    ISBN 0-02-864621-5 (alk. paper)
    1. Nix, Don, 1941–   . 2. Rock musicians—United States—

Biography. 3. Cookery.   I. Title.
ML420.N713A3   1997
782.42166'092—dc20

                                        96-27474

                                        CIP

                                        MN

FOR KATRINA

ROAD MAP

vii

viii

FOREWORD

I hope this foreword isn't going to delay you too much in getting to the meat and potatoes of this fine volume, but as the author and I happen to be the very closest of friends, it seemed an appropriate request on his part to have me write a little something by way of an appetizer.

The memory of how we met is particularly clear even though it is now over twenty years ago. I was planning to record my umpteenth album to celebrate a decade of professional blues making and wanted to have an independent producer at the helm who would contribute new ideas and give me a fresh musical perspective. To that end I had my manager do the phone fingering to hunt for a gentleman called Don Nix (a name I knew only from reading the credits on Freddie King's latest LP and finding he not only produced it but wrote the hit song "Going Down," which has since gone on to be regarded as a blues classic). How could we go wrong?

I consulted with my drummer and good friend Keef Hartley about the choice, and we both agreed to have him come out to Los Angeles from his home base of Memphis to begin recording us. When I introduced myself to Don by telephone, he sounded as if he'd enjoy the trip, so, with the blessings of management, deal makers, and Polygram Records, we were all set to go with flight arrival details in hand and ticket paid for.

Now Keef and I assumed we'd be identifiable from various album photos, but we had no idea what Don looked like. Nevertheless, on the appointed day Keef and I went to Los Angeles Airport to welcome him at the gate, and, as a flamboyant sartorial gesture, Keef got decked out in full Navajo Indian gear minus bow and arrows and headdress while I fashioned a clerical collar from white cardboard atop a black tee shirt until, with hair slicked down flat, I presented the appearance of a legitimate man of the cloth. We stood there scanning the passengers as they emerged and finally zeroed in on the person in U.S. Army battle fatigues who could only have been our new producer. With great confidence, we expansively stretched out our hands and smiled broadly at the approaching guy until, with a stab of embarrassing idiocy, we realized it was the wrong man! With eyes focused straight ahead, the soldier walked right past us.

Keef and I looked at each other trying to regain some sort of dignity (dressed as we were) and wondered what to do next when from behind our backs a hysterical roar of laughter broke out. The military looking guy was now pointing at us and cracking up at the totally bewildered

Don Nix and John Mayall on the road, c. 1980.
Photo: Mike Gardner.

x

expressions on our faces. Of course, it was Don, and from that time on we became as close as the Three Musketeers (or, in our sillier moments, the Three Stooges).

Not the funniest anecdote in the world, I'll be the first to admit, but, then again this isn't my book. What you are about to get stuck into is the reminiscences of a truly humorous raconteur and participant in an exciting period of rock 'n' roll that might have slipped your attention. Here you will find stories of the road that tell of an era of our musical history that will hopefully give you something to remember and have you on the phone urging your friends to go out and buy it.

As if this memoir isn't enough, you are also getting a cookbook full of recipes from a whole slew of musicians who often don't get to eat as handsomely on the road as they do in their own kitchens. Well then, that's it from me.

In summation, I'll put it to you this way: If the tales don't tickle your funny bone, the recipes should tickle your palate. It doesn't get any better than that!

JOHN MAYALL
SEPTEMBER 1995

PRELUDE

The Memphis music scene has become a phenomenon with literary midgets as well as giants doing interviews, taking notes, and writing books. The trouble with this is, of course, if you ask twenty people the same question, you get twenty different answers, twenty points of view, twenty different memories, and, in some cases, people who were on the fringe or who were not there at all, giving their opinions about what happened. I have read books and heard people interviewed about Stax and its glory days when I know damn well they never set foot in the place. I get angry sometimes when people look at it from an analytical point of view. They put it under a microscope, dissect it, examine it, and reexamine it. They try to make it something it ain't, cause when you get past all the books and labels, it was just people trying to make a living the best they could. Creating something that had never been before without even knowing it. People who got paid very little for what they contributed but would have done it for free because they loved it. Making music meant freedom as well as a sense of belonging, but most of all it was fun.

MEMPHIS: THE TRIP BEGINS

I hated being alone on rainy nights. I had called every female I had known since the second grade with no luck whatsoever. It probably didn't help that I was extremely high and it was well past midnight. I got into the white Rolls and drove down the long driveway onto Central Avenue in the heart of Chickasaw Gardens, the most fashionable neighborhood in Memphis. I owned one of the oldest homes in the gardens, with three Rolls Royces and a '65 'Vette parked in the four-car garage. I had more money in the bank than I could ever hope to spend, all the things I had always thought it took to be really happy. But I was miserable and, even worse, I was bored. I drove around for several hours washing Percodan down with Remy Martin, which put me in a nostalgic mood. I drove out to the neighborhood I had grown up in and past my old house on Deerwood Cove, and ended up sitting on the steps of the high school I had attended, wondering what the hell had happened to the past twenty years.

THE NEW DEAL

In the fall of 1955, we had returned to school armed with a new music. Rockabilly, rock 'n' roll, rhythm and blues, or whatever you called it was definitely not the music of our parents, grandparents, or anyone else who took refuge in the sounds of Snooky Lanson, Teresa Brewer, or the Andrews Sisters. But it changed more than just our listening habits. It changed our attitudes, the way we dressed, and the way our elders looked at us. I went to Messick High School in Memphis, where just the year before Elvis had come to play our Wednesday morning assembly program, and where Dewey Phillips could be heard nightly playing everything from Sister Rosetta Tharpe to Hank Ballard and the Midnighters. Dewey's radio show, *Red Hot and Blue,* was our connection to the new culture and we never missed it. I had met Donald "Duck" Dunn and Steve Cropper in elementary school. We were from working-class families and, although they were close-knit, we were bored. We spent our afternoons and evenings playing baseball, shooting snooker, or playing pin-

Don Nix, left, and Donald "Duck" Dunn, 1958.

ball. We had paper routes, mowed lawns, or did other odd jobs to finance our pastimes. Although we had not yet thought about learning to play an instrument or trying our hand at singing, we *dressed* the part. Elvis and all the rockabilly cats bought their clothes on Beale Street, so that's where we shopped. Our favorite store was Lansky Brothers, where we went to buy peg pants and shirts, skinny belts, and of course shoes of the bluest suede.

I think there were two major reasons to cause us to think seriously about getting into music. The first was the discovery of Arkansas road-houses like the Cotton Club, Danny's Club, and our favorite, the Plan-tation Inn, located across the river in West Memphis. Black singers and musicians like Willie Mitchell, Al Jackson, the Del Rios, "Sissy" Charles Turner, and the Veltones played all night while we sat and soaked up our first taste of live R&B and doo-wop. The second reason was the discovery that we didn't have to shake like Elvis or have his dark good looks to meet girls. That point was driven home by the first appearance of Buddy Holly on the Ed Sullivan show. There was old Buddy up there singing and playing, ugly as a stick and stiff as a board, but all the girls were screaming. The common denominator was the music. It dawned on us: In order to get girls, we needed guitars, and we needed them quick.

After talking our parents into cosigning for our instruments, we were off in search of someone with amps, drums, and, most importantly, a garage to practice in. We found a drummer in Melvin Tolbert and a garage and amp man by the name of Mike Leach, who later became one of Memphis and Nashville's top arrangers and bass players. While Cropper was busy taking lessons from a jazz guitarist named Sid Manker and practicing alone in the privacy of his home, Duck, Melvin, and I banged away nightly in Mike's garage trying to learn the hits of the day like Link Wray's "Rumble," Little Walter's "My Babe," and Bill Doggett's "Honky Tonk." Our first paying gig was at the Bethel LaBelle Canteen in East Memphis for five bucks apiece. We must have sounded terrible playing the same six songs over and over. But since there weren't that many bands around, the audience had no one to compare us to and they loved it. After that first gig I didn't sleep for a week. Hell, I was show people, headed for the cosmos never to return. At least that was the plan.

Our first gig, Memphis, 1958. Left to right: Duck Dunn, Melvin Tolbert, Don Nix.

In our senior year, Duck, Melvin, and I went our separate ways. Duck, who had been playing guitar, bought an electric bass and joined Cropper, Charlie Freeman, and Terry Johnson in a group they called the Royal Spades. Melvin got a day job and I joined the army. I had gotten discouraged with trying to do well in school, which I never did, and trying my best to master the guitar, which also evaded me. In those days, it was standard practice for guys who were dissatisfied with their lot to join the army. "Yeah, that's the answer," I thought. Fort Jackson, South Carolina, in the winter was a nightmare, but it also opened my eyes to a lot of things. To escape the boredom and loneliness of army life, I started to read, something I had never done; not even in school did I read a complete book. First I read *Catcher in the Rye,* followed by Jack Kerouac's *On the Road.* They had a profound effect on me and I read parts of them over and over. I also knew that I could never do manual labor for a living, something that might sound a bit cheeky now, but when you're 18 you think things like that. I also swore to myself that for the rest of my life I would sleep as late as I wanted, eat what I wanted, and generally do as I pleased without taking orders from anyone. If you're gonna dream, you might as well do it right. Amen!

I got out of the army in July 1960 and returned to Memphis, where the Royal Spades had become one of the hottest bands around. Best in music, worst in name. Charles "Packey" Axton had bought a tenor sax and started rehearsing with the band. Packey was a madman and had been drinking since the age of 14, a fact that fully qualified him for the Royal Spades. They had a regular job playing a roadhouse in Millington called Neil's Hideaway. Since none of them sang, they had also hired a singer by the name of Ronnie Stoots, who went by the name Ronnie Angel. Neil's attracted a strange mixture of patrons, high school and college students from Memphis and locals from the county who worked hard all day and came to Neil's at night to relax and drink beer by the quart. They left their teeth at home, and I was deathly afraid of them. The band's music had a strange effect on the locals. They were used to hearing their music on the jukebox, and the live music soothed some tired brows while it drove others completely crazy. Fights and flying bottles were common occurrences, and the band quickly learned when to duck and when to cover.

Watching my best friends play and having a good time finally got the best of me, and in the fall of 1960 it was decided I would join the band if I purchased a saxophone. Some white bands around town had one horn player, but none of them had two. So again I went to my mother to cosign a note for an alto saxophone. After mumbling something about the Les Paul Jr. under the bed gathering dust, she did, and I was in. Thank God for the unwritten law at that time: In the South, no mother could deny a request from her oldest son. Packey and I worked out riffs we had picked up from the black bands we had watched in West Memphis, especially Willie Mitchell. Willie had the tightest five-piece band I have ever seen, even to this day. Besides Willie on trumpet he had James Lupor on tenor sax, Joe Hall on piano, Lewis Steinberg on bass, and the great Al Jackson on drums. They were awe-inspiring and we couldn't get enough. We followed them from club to club, begging the owners (who knew we were underage) to let us in to watch the band. The clubs in Arkansas didn't care how old you were as long as you had the price of admission, but in Memphis age restrictions were a lot tighter.

Memphis in 1960 was a long way from integration, and the black musicians could not mingle with the patrons of an all-white club. So we followed them to the storage room, kitchen, or sometimes even the parking lot—wherever they were banished to on their breaks. Not only were they the best band we had ever heard, they were also the nicest, taking time to answer our questions about this riff or that change or the way they communicated on the bandstand. With seven people, we sometimes argued on stage about what song we would do next, while Willie and his guys (without speaking or even looking at each other) flowed easily from one number to the next. Damn, they were cool and we wanted to be just like them.

Also about this time, we decided to change the name of the band to the Marquis, but since no one ever pronounced it correctly we simplified it to the Mar-Keys. We began playing bigger and better engagements around the midsouth area, university dances, high school proms, and, of course, the clubs. We played the Hi Hat, the Starlight, Clear Pool, The Rainbow Room, and black clubs like Currie's Tropicana, where it was our turn to sit our breaks out in the kitchen.

About the time the Mar-Keys were gaining popularity, Packey's mom, Estelle Axton, and her brother, Jim Stewart, rented an old movie theater in a rundown neighborhood in a mostly black section of South Memphis at 926 East McLemore. The theater's old marquee still flashed *CAPITOL* in red neon. The seats were taken out and one side of the building was partitioned, leaving a huge high-ceilinged room whose floor was slanted at a 20-degree angle toward the screen. The screen was removed and the back section of the theater was also partitioned, making way for the control room area. Jim Stewart, who worked at First Tennessee Bank

Eddie Floyd and Jim Stewart, Memphis, 1968.
Photo: Don Nix.

as a teller, took charge of the studio, and Mrs. Axton opened a record shop in the front of the building, which was the former lobby and concession stand of the old theater. She named the shop Satellite Records and it quickly became the hit of the neighborhood. Everybody came in to see Mrs. Axton hold court and play the latest R&B and blues hits. They all liked her and she them, and the record shop became a hangout for all the local kids, disc jockeys, and every member of the Mar-Keys. The studio became our second home and Mrs. Axton our second mother.

Every morning as soon as I woke, I went to the studio to meet the rest of the band. By this time I had bought a baritone sax. Being 6'1", I had been teased by members of the band about playing a toy saxophone, because the alto was so small. They said it looked funny, but I paid them no mind until audience members at local gigs began voicing the same opinions. Remember, in order to meet girls, you didn't have to play that well—you just had to look cool doing it, so the alto quickly took its place under the bed with the Les Paul Jr. I hated the bari. It was heavy and took a lot more wind than the alto to play. I really wanted to play tenor, but since Packey already had that covered, I was once again stuck with an instrument I would never master. Charlie Freeman quit the band to join a small orchestra from Arkansas to play the hotels and clubs along the Gulf Coast. We then hired Wayne Jackson on trumpet to fill out our

SOULSVILLE
U.S.A.

Homer Banks in front of Stax
Studios, "Soulsville, U.S.A.,"
showing old movie theater
marquee, 1968.
Photo: Don Nix.

horn section. Wayne had studied music and knew all the old standards and helped Packey and me with harmony parts. He became our arranger and we started adding jazz tunes to our play list: songs by Bobby Timmons, Mose Allison, and Cannonball Adderly. Wayne was from West Memphis and was more aggressive than any of us. On stage he became the front man, something none of us had ever wanted to do. Wayne even sang a few songs, something I had been doing for a couple of months. Even Cropper sang an occasional Jimmy Reed number. But Ronnie was still the main vocalist. Terry Johnson was the only one still in high school and we had to wait every day until he got out to start rehearsing. Terry had become one of the best drummers around, and despite his age, his shuffle had become second only to that of his mentor, Al Jackson.

While waiting for him every day, we explored the old theater building where there were many nooks and crannies for restless youths who had plenty of time on their hands. We hung out in the record shop, listening to the latest hits with the locals, or went next door to a run-down neighborhood beer bar called Mae's Grill. Mae was a nice old woman who smoked and drank too much. She had massive mood swings and heard voices from beyond the grave. We were her only patrons. But finally things got so weird that even we stopped going in. One morning she failed to show up to open the bar and we never saw her again. Mae's Grill eventually became East Music Publishing Offices, part of the Stax Record family. On the other side of the studio was a barber shop where Carl Cunningham, a small black kid, shined shoes. He later became a fantastic drummer with the Bar Kays and died in the plane crash with Otis Redding. On the other side of the barber shop was the Weona food store, where Duck and I ate crackers and thick slices of bologna for lunch. These shops, too, became future offices for Stax Records. The corner of College and McLemore became our world, where blacks, whites, shopkeepers, and teenage rock 'n' rollers all got along. At least for a while.

DADDY'O DEWEY

The record shop became a gathering place for local disc jockeys like Rufus Thomas from WDIA and Dewey Phillips, who was between jobs at that time. Dewey was a maniac and we had never met anyone like him. Dewey had been my music guru in high school and I seldom missed his nightly radio show, *Red Hot and Blue.* He had been one of the top disc jockeys in the country and by far the best in the South. He played everything

Dewey Phillips at WHBQ.

from Gene Vincent to Muddy Waters, Jimmy Reed to Danny and the Juniors. He did and said outrageous things on the air, and his show was a lot more entertaining than watching TV. Dewey did a great impression of Dizzy Dean and carried on conversations with himself as Diz and Dewey. He put records of the same song like "Hound Dog" or "Tutti Frutti" on two turntables and try to play them in sync (something that was virtually impossible to do). He played Elvis's or Jerry Lee's new releases twenty or more times in a row. When he left WHBQ, Elvis took him to Hollywood to become one of the Memphis mafia, but things quickly got out of hand. At a big movie industry dinner thrown in Elvis's honor, Dewey tapped his water glass with his butter knife, stood up, and began one of those long, insane monologues that only he understood. To say that Elvis was humiliated was probably an understatement. But the final straw came when, after dinner, Dewey was introduced to Yul Brynner, a man not noted for his sense of humor and more than just a little self-conscious about his diminutive stature. Dewey looked him up and down and said loudly, "You're a little ol' bitty thang, ain't ya?" Needless to say Dewey didn't last long in Tinsel Town. He was a marked man and returned to Memphis broke and jobless.

Dewey had been seriously injured in a car accident when he was younger and he walked with a slight limp. This led to on-again off-again addictions to speed and painkillers for the rest of his life, which I'm sure didn't help his manic behavior. By the time he started hanging out

ROAD STORIES AND RECIPES

at the studio, he was a broken man showing up in the dead of winter in a T-shirt and house slippers. Sometimes he came in so high that I was sure he was going to chew his lips off. Dewey and Packey quickly became close friends since both enjoyed higher altitudes, and they set up shop upstairs in the theater's old projection booth. Dewey introduced Packey to Robitussin cough syrup, which in those days contained a small amount of codeine, and they made daily pilgrimages to an old drugstore down the street for a bottle of "Robo." One day, somebody up in Washington decided Robitussin could not be purchased without a doctor's prescription. This decision was made without notifying Dewey or Packey, so when they dropped in the next morning for their daily supply, they were horrified at the news. They regrouped back at the record shop to plan their next move. They were not going to take this lying down. The Civil Rights movement was having great success with sit-ins, so Packey and Dewey thought maybe a cough-in would do the trick. Off they went back to the drugstore, where they sat on the floor coughing their heads off. But the old druggist was having none of it and, when he emerged from behind the counter with a baseball bat, Packey had seen enough and beat a hasty retreat. Dewey was much more committed and, because of his gimp leg, a lot slower. He took the full impact of the old man's anger and his baseball bat. Hospitalized for a week with head injuries and arrested for trespassing, Dewey took another giant step toward the bottom.

After his hospital stay, Dewey returned to the studio with his head swathed in bandages and a new prescription for Percodan in his pocket. He promised Mrs. Axton he would be good and not cause any more trouble. He kept his promise for a week or two, but late one afternoon after being awake for a couple of days, he crashed in the projection room on an old army cot that Packey had provided for such occasions. He woke about midnight to find himself locked in. The only window opened out onto the Capitol marquee from the upstairs projection booth. Dewey was desperate and crawled out the small opening. Once on the marquee, he stuck his head through the neon *O* and began calling out to five black youths who were having a late night doo-wop session on the corner. "Hey Elvis!" Dewey shouted. Dewey called everybody Elvis. The singing stopped, but the group had no idea where the voice was coming from. So they started singing again. "Hey Elvis!" came the voice again. The singing stopped, but still no one. Finally, after the third "Hey Elvis!" one of the guys looked skyward, where he spotted Dewey's terrified face sticking through the marquee. One of the group was William C. Brown

III, who later became one of the Mad-Lads, the great Stax recording group. He happened to know Mrs. Axton and went home and called her. She had been asleep for hours, but drove from East Memphis in her housecoat to let Dewey out. He was so thankful to be out of that dark, cavernous building that he didn't even ask her for a ride home; he just vanished in the night. Mrs. Axton really liked Dewey, but her patience was wearing thin. The last straw came a few days later when, in the crowded record shop, Dewey laid a tremendous fart, yelling "Whoa Elvis!" and tried to blame it on her. He was gone, never to return.

Dewey almost recovered a few times over the next ten years, with occasional jobs at small radio stations in and around Memphis, but the pain and the pills drove him crazy. He fantasized about getting back together with Elvis or any of his old record or showbiz friends, who had all disowned him. One night while driving home from a late-night recording session, I found Dewey standing under a street lamp in the middle of the road in a pouring rainstorm. He was living with his mother on Macon Street and I begged him to go back in the house and sleep it off. He was dressed in rags, held together by dozens of small safety pins, and was way too wired to think about sleep. He wanted me to take him to the other side of town to meet Elvis at Chenault's Restaurant, a place he often rented for private parties. I finally agreed, after realizing Dewey was not in the mood to take no for an answer. I drove him to the restaurant, not knowing if Elvis was there or not. One thing I did know was if he *was* there, no way was he going to let Dewey in. As we pulled in to the back parking lot, Dewey spotted Elvis's white Lincoln in the pouring rain. He got out, thanked me for the ride, and made his way across the parking lot, missing most of the mud holes to the back entrance. He was inside for less than 30 seconds. I drove him back home in silence, something rare for Dewey. By the time we got back to his mother's, it had stopped raining, and I watched him disappear into the dark doorway. That was the last time I saw Dewey alive. He died in his sleep four days later.

11

A GUY COULD GET KILLED

Up to this point we had been unscathed playing rowdy bars and road-houses. But that all changed one warm spring evening at the Tropical Room, a real dive located on highway 78 south of Memphis. Some of us had been sitting with two young ladies on our breaks, just passing time and nothing else. It turned out that one of them was married and her husband was the jealous kind who stayed drunk a lot. Even at our young age we knew that that was not a winning combination. Evidently, he had come looking for her and spotted us sitting at her table. Being outnumbered, he retreated to the parking lot to lie in wait.

Like the gentlemen we were, after the last set, we walked the young ladies to their car. Most of the patrons had already gone and the parking lot was dark and empty. There was one other car parked beside the ladies', and guess who popped out? He was drunk, mad, and ready to fight, but we convinced him he was no match for the seven of us (or so we thought). He returned to his car and opened the door, but instead of getting in he reached into the back seat and came out with a rifle, screaming something about killing us all. All loyalties were off. It was every man for himself and we scattered like crows. That is, all except Packey, who was never known for his speed, especially after five hours in a roadhouse where cold beverages were served.

Apparently the guy had a weak moment and instead of shooting him, he swung the rifle by the stock, striking Packey above the left eye with the barrel. This caused the rifle to discharge and Packey went down. Fortunately, the bullet missed, something we didn't know at the time. Duck and I ran into the club screaming, "He shot Packey. The son of a bitch shot Packey!" There were a couple of sheriff's deputies there, and they immediately ran out and disarmed the guy. They handcuffed him and led him to their car, where they were frisking him when Packey came stumbling out of the dark, blood pouring down his face. He was shaking his fist in the air screaming, "Book him! Book him!"

By this time, there were two more squad cars on the scene, and as they were putting this guy in one of them, Packey walked up and punched him. I guess Packey figured that after all this guy had put him through he at least deserved one punch, even though the guy was handcuffed. Unfortunately, the cops didn't see it that way. They grabbed Packey, cuffed him, and took them both to jail. Our loyalties returned, and we all spent the night trying to get him out. Most of us were still up the next morning when he was set free.

LAST NIGHT

Mrs. Axton hocked her house to buy an Ampex mono recording machine. Because Jim had a small studio in Brunswick, Tennessee, he already had mikes and a small mixing console. Chips Moman put most of the control room together, because Jim still worked at the bank and

The Mar-Keys, 1961, in the Stax studio. <u>Left to right:</u> Packey Axton, Wayne Jackson, Duck Dunn (obscured), Don Nix, Terry Johnson, Steve Cropper, Jerry Lee "Smoochie" Smith.
Ernest C. Withers, photographer, "Pictures Tell the Story," Memphis.

could only help at night and on the weekends. The first recording sessions were local white artists like Nick Charles and Charles Hines, with the Mar-Keys playing on most of these recordings, but outside of some local airplay nothing much was happening until the day Rufus Thomas brought in his 17-year-old daughter, Carla. They recorded a duo called "Cause I Love You," which was a moderate hit. Carla recorded "Gee Whiz" a few months later and it became an instant smash, although I don't think anybody expected one so soon. Atlantic Records' vice president, Jerry Wexler, flew down and signed a distribution deal with Jim and Mrs. Axton and, because the name of the record shop was Satellite, that was also the name of the label. However, when "Gee Whiz" was released it was on the Atlantic label.

The studio was still used mainly as our rehearsal hall, where by now other musicians from the neighborhood were dropping by with their instruments. Since there were not many recording sessions going on in

ROAD STORIES AND RECIPES

those days, great jam sessions went on all day and sometimes into the night. It was during one of these sessions that "Last Night" was recorded. Chips had turned on the recorder when he thought he had heard something different, although no one else shared his enthusiasm. That is, no one except Mrs. Axton, who took an acetate of the session up to the record shop and began playing it nonstop. Almost everyone who came in wanted to buy it. She was begging Jim to release it, but Jim was careful and didn't think such a simple tune would ever do anything, and besides, there was no B-side. Mrs. Axton got us together and told us to go in and cut another song, something that would make a compatible flipside for "Last Night." We went into the studio and recorded "The Night Before" a few days later.

Mrs. Axton was determined, and in the spring of 1961 "Last Night" by the Mar-Keys was released. Although distributed by Atlantic, this record was released on the Satellite label and it was Mrs. Axton's baby. At her request, every disc jockey in Memphis, white and black, was playing it. It soon spread to other southern cities like Little Rock, Arkansas, Jackson, Mississippi, and especially Birmingham, Alabama, where it quickly went to number one on the local charts. "Last Night" was going to be a big record and everyone knew it. At last we were going on the road and we were going to be rich and famous. Our wildest dreams were coming true. But if we had known what lay ahead we probably would have gotten day jobs and stayed at home.

Because "Last Night" was such a hit in Birmingham, we made our first road trip there. Mrs. Axton cosigned the note for a new Chevy Greenbriar van and we were off, promising to be careful and keep up the notes. It was a beautiful summer morning and I'll never forget how excited we were to be finally on the road. We had added a piano player by the name of Jerry Lee "Smoochie" Smith at Mrs. Axton's insistence because he had played on the record. That made a four-piece rhythm section, a three-piece horn section, one vocalist, and all our luggage and instruments piled into one tiny van. There we were headed through northern Mississippi down highway 72 on our first adventure, and if ignorance is bliss we had to be the happiest truckload of people in the world.

We arrived in the late afternoon, checked in to our motel, and headed for the gig. The promoter was a local disc jockey who held weekly Saturday night dances for teenagers and young adults. The place was packed and we were ready. Since we hadn't had time to have any publicity photos taken, everyone assumed we were black. They had never seen white boys play R&B and they loved it. So did we. After being paid we went back to the motel where, too excited to sleep, we just sat up and talked. About 1:00 there was a knock at the door. Someone opened it and there was the disc jockey, a fifth of whiskey, a case of beer, and a deck of cards in his hands. The next morning we were on our way home, tired, broke, and a little bit wiser. But we had learned a few basic rules of the road: Always be prompt, play as hard as you can, and never, under any circumstances, play poker with the promoter's deck.

We were used to being broke since none of us had ever had over $100.00 at one time. My father drove a truck for a small cleaners, Duck's father drove a cab, and Cropper's dad was a railroad detective. Steve was an only child, Duck had four brothers and two sisters, and I had a brother, Larry, and a sister, Kitty. My father always left for work before we woke and did not return until the late evening. It was left to my mother to run the household and I have always been very close to her. Not only did she cosign for my instruments, she encouraged me in my musical endeavors. She was completely devoted to her children; I remember once she delivered my morning paper route in freezing weather when I was too sick to go. My mother was beautiful, with dark skin and black hair, evidence of her Cherokee Indian heritage. My great-grandfather was half-Cherokee and had served in the 5th South Carolina Cavalry during the Civil War. He moved his family to Tennessee in 1882 and farmed the land around Troy in Obion County, ninety miles north of Memphis. My mother and father were from very large families, each of them having eleven siblings. My father grew up during the Depression in northern Mississippi, which was probably not the best place to be at that time. He had little education and had to work twelve hours a day, six days a week to support us. Like a lot of fathers of that era, he didn't get to spend much time with us. I didn't think about it much then, but since his sudden death in 1980, it's something I think about every day.

Coming home from our first road trip without any money was something I think everyone expected, except us. But it didn't get us down. So the next week we were off again, this time to Bossier City, Louisiana. Just across the river from Shreveport, Bossier was not a city at all, but a mile and a half of the nastiest nightclubs and roadhouses you have ever seen. At the top of the strip of clubs, strip joints, and beer bars was the Showbar, where we were booked for five days. Across the highway was the Kick-a-Poo Motel, which was home to waitresses, musicians, hookers, and barflys from the area. We played behind the bar, elevated some six feet above the room. In the rear was a strip club, where we were not allowed because of our age. However, during a break on our second night we discovered we could sneak upstairs behind the sound booth and observe all the T and A we could stand.

One of the strippers was the famous Crystal Brite, whose companion on stage was a defumed skunk. Crystal was a school teacher for nine months of the year and made her living the other three as a stripper. She was the first stripper to dance topless and we were glad to know her. She had the room next to Duck's and mine at the Kick-a-Poo. One afternoon while I was sleeping late, he got the skunk and placed it on my stomach. He knew I hated that skunk, defumed or not. I awoke looking eye to eye with that dreadful little animal and ran screaming into the parking lot, my bare ass shining in the afternoon sun.

16

Rufus Thomas in Estelle Axton's record store next door to Stax Records, 1962.
Photo: Don Nix.

That week, "Last Night" broke nationwide. Our booking agent, Ray Brown, called to tell us that we were to appear on Dick Clark's *American Bandstand* the following Thursday. Ray's company, National Artist Attractions, booked Ace Cannon, Jerry Lee Lewis, Rufus Thomas, the Mar-Keys, and other local acts. Ray was a former disc jockey for WMPS in Memphis. He would book his mother into the restroom of the Greyhound bus station if he could make a buck on it. Back then, we trusted everyone, knowing nothing about kickbacks or double bookings, something Ray did often. That Saturday night, our last night at the Showbar, we bade farewell to Crystal, her skunk, and various friends we had made that week and headed back to Memphis. Sleeping all day Sunday, we left Monday morning accompanied by Carla Thomas, with Mrs. Axton as chaperone. We stopped in St. Louis that afternoon for a local radio show and then drove to Saginaw, Michigan, for a show with us and Carla on Tuesday night.

The show was another disc jockey sock hop. The place was packed, and during our set the crowd was well-behaved. But when Carla came on, the place went crazy, with people rushing the stage, something that was completely unexpected. We all panicked and ran for our lives, all except for Carla, who stood her ground and finished the show with just the rhythm section.

There were ten people traveling in the van, which was way too many. Terry Johnson, Wayne, and I rode the bus from Saginaw to Detroit for the next show on Wednesday night. The rest of the band dropped Carla and Mrs. Axton off at a motel and then drove down to Greyhound to pick us up. While they waited for us inside the terminal, the cops towed the van and we walked out to find an empty parking space. This was downtown and we walked a few blocks to the police station to bail our truck out. The cops now had eight Southern white boys and they couldn't believe their luck. After locking us in a room for a couple of hours, they put us through the usual jive-ass cop routine, charged us an outrageous amount of money, and gave us our van back. Packey had always hated the North and had never trusted Yankees. This incident reinforced his hatred and left a bad taste in all of us for that part of the country.

The show that night was fantastic, with Don Covay, Wilbert Harrison, the original Shirelles, Don & Juan, Carla, and us. This show too was all-black, with just our eight white faces. The audience gave us a tremendous reception and we left that night feeling there were at least a few nice people in Detroit. We drove all night and the next day to arrive just in time for the afternoon *American Bandstand* show.

17

ROAD STORIES AND RECIPES

AMERICAN BANDSTAND

We had watched *American Bandstand* all during high school and imagined it to be a magic place where all the neighborhood high school kids came to dance and hang out with Dick, Frankie, Fabian, and all the gang. We weren't ready for the huge TV complex underneath the elevated train in a rundown Philly neighborhood, but we were still excited about being on national TV.

The first hint of trouble came after we were ushered through the side door and into the studio, where Dick Clark greeted us. Smoochie was headed straight for him with his hand out and, before we could head him off, he was telling Dick, "You're a lot shorter than you look on TV." By this time we all knew that Smoochie had become a liability and his days were numbered. The damage was done, and Dick walked back to his podium and started leafing through the day's script, without shaking hands with the rest of us.

In those days, *Bandstand* was the zenith in rock-'n'-roll TV viewing, running an hour and a half from 3:00 to 4:30 every weekday. There were usually two guests per show and on this day, besides us, the great Bobby "Blue" Bland was there. Bobby recorded for Don Robey's Peacock label in Houston, Texas, and although we knew he was from Memphis, we had never met him. We even did a couple of his songs, "Saint James Infirmary" and "Turn on Your Love Light." He was accompanied that day by Little Junior Parker and Junior's father. Of course we were in awe and followed them downstairs, where we sat in a dressing room talking and drinking wine. About forty-five minutes before the show, Junior, his daddy, and Packey went out for some more wine, while we went upstairs to set up for the show. The audience was let in, cameras were rolled into place, and *American Bandstand* was on the air. Bobby Bland was to appear in the first thirty-minute segment and we were to appear forty-five minutes later in the last segment of the show. We passed the time by watching the action on a monitor backstage.

All at once it was our time to go. We gathered behind the *American Bandstand* logo, as directed by the stage manager. Packey, however, was nowhere to be found. Duck, Wayne, and I scattered looking everywhere for him. At the last minute, we found him downstairs with Junior Parker and his dad, so drunk they couldn't have found each other's ass with a search warrant. We got Packey upstairs and into position, but remember, this was live television and there were no retakes. Wayne, Packey, and I were in front, the horn line. We had worked up a few steps to go along with "Last Night," but I didn't feel that Packey was up to any dancing. He could barely stand and we smelled disaster. Right before Dick introduced us I leaned over and told Packey, "Don't move. No matter what happens, stay put." He looked at me with that silly drunken grin on his face and acknowledged my instructions. "Ladies and gentlemen, the Mar-Keys," Dick announced as he came out of a commercial, and we were on.

Of course we weren't really playing live, but pantomiming the record (which wasn't turned up very loud, making it hard to get into the spirit of things). It also made it evident to the studio audience that something was bad wrong. There we were out front, me and Wayne on either side of Packey, doing those silly little dance steps while old Packey just stood there weaving. He looked like one of those plastic punching dummies with sand in the bottom: No matter how far over it goes, it always comes back standing straight. It was time for the tenor sax solo. I had to give him a poke in the ribs with my elbow. It was even worse than I had thought. Packey actually blew the solo, and I think the lack of oxygen this caused made things even worse. I remember thinking, "Two more verses Lord, just two more verses. Please don't let Packey fall down on national television." But it didn't look good. Packey's feet were not moving, and by this time he was weaving uncontrollably. "He's going over. He's going to fall. Oh God he's gonna fall and there's nothing I can do about it." I started making plans for that awful moment. Should I stay and help him up, making some lame excuse about low blood sugar? Or should I run, run like the wind, out the side door up to the el, take the train to the Greyhound station, and go home and get a real job? I had already set my mind on the latter when the music started to fade and the song was over. "Thank you, oh thank you Lord. Now we can get out of here."

But Dick wanted to talk and motioned us out to the middle of the studio, where he stood mike in hand with that big shit-eatin' grin he always wore. He had us. We had to do it and we walked over to him reluctantly. The walk was about eight or ten feet and, after we gathered around, I noticed him looking over my shoulder with a puzzled expression. I turned around to find Packey still standing back where I had told him: not moving no matter what. Steve saw it too and we scooted together shoulder-to-shoulder to obscure Dick's view of the still-grinning Packey, weaving back and forth like some mad walkin' Charlie. The producer had asked Duck and Terry Johnson before the show to recall some anecdote that had occurred during our travels that we could share with Mr. Clark. They were still laughing about the skunk they had put in my room the week before in Bossier City, the only trouble being they forgot to tell him who the skunk belonged to and of course didn't say a word to me about any of it. So imagine my surprise when after asking our names, and where we lived, Dick stuck the microphone in my face and asked, very concerned, "Now what's this I hear about a skunk in your room?" Well I started relating my stripper/skunk/motel story when I saw Dick's jaw go slack and the famous smile quickly disappeared. I was just getting to the good part when he suddenly withdrew the microphone and told us how nice it was for us to drive such a long way to be on the show, and then we were gone. I don't know who was more relieved, us or Dick. Needless to say, we weren't asked back for a repeat performance.

Mrs. Axton and Carla had had enough, and the next morning they flew back to Memphis. We had dreamed of playing at some beautiful beach during the summer, the reason being sun, surf, and, of course, girls—the main reason we were doing all of this anyway. Don't get me wrong, we loved the music and we loved to play, but we could play at home. We wanted some girls and we wanted them now.

None of us had a violent nature. In fact, we were about as nonviolent as you could get. We thought of ourselves more as lovers than fighters, and avoided trouble at any cost. We had had our share of fights during school, but bad-ass roadhogs we were not. Growing up in Memphis was bad enough, seeing people cut, shot, and beat up beyond belief. Memphis, like any river town, had its mean side and was not a place to make any quick moves. I think watching black bands like Willie Mitchell, Ben Branch and the Largos, and Bowlegs Miller helped develop our stage demeanor. They were so cool on the bandstand that when drunk rednecks got on the stage they just let them make fools of themselves until the bouncers came to throw them out. They let their music do their talking, something we tried to emulate.

We had told our booking agent before we left about our desire to frolic on the beach that summer. So on our way to Philly, we did just that. After finishing *Bandstand*, we headed for Virginia Beach, Virginia, for a week's stay at Moose's Tropicana right on the beach. We rented a house next door to the club. We were ready to party and, for the next week, that's exactly what we did, sleeping 'til mid-afternoon, getting up, eating, and going to the beach before setting up to play that night. The club was packed every night with good crowds who liked our music. After the gig, we'd hang out on the pier all night, watching the locals fish for sharks. We stayed out there and watched the sun come up, then to bed to start the cycle all over again. We had a great week and even got paid, although when it came time to pay up, the club owner wanted to flip a coin, double or nothing. When I asked him whose coin we would use, he replied, "Mine, of course." We took our pay and left.

MYRTLE BEACH

The next stop was Myrtle Beach, South Carolina, for a week at the Beach Club, which sat in a grove of pine trees north of town just across the highway from the ocean. We were following the Five Royales, who had played the week before, and we knew we had our work cut out for us. We played every night to packed houses filled with college kids, vacationers, and beach bums. The beaches in this part of the country are some of the most beautiful on the East Coast, and although we still stayed out all night and watched the sun come up every morning, we started getting up a little earlier to spend more time by the sea. Things were good; things were real good.

One night I went with some locals to Atlantic Beach, a few miles up the coast. They wanted to take me to a club run by a crazed Jerry Lee Lewis fanatic. This place was right on the beach, built like a giant flying saucer (appropriately named The Flying Saucer Club) and covered in the gaudiest of neon. There was no band, just a jukebox filled with Jerry Lee Lewis and Roy Orbison records, and The Killer's picture was everywhere. I took one look at the owner and wanted to leave immediately. He was a big guy, wearing one of those cheap Hawaiian shirts, with dyed blonde hair combed just like his hero. I felt like I had just stepped into the Twilight Zone. Although the place was supposed to stay open until dawn, there were only a few people, so he closed early, but not too soon for me. He closed the place by reaching under the bar, grabbing a .38 pistol, and firing four shots into the ceiling. That shut her down real quick. As we were walking back across the beach one of the locals asked me, "Did you take a look at the holes in that damn ceiling? There must have been a thousand of them." I told him, "No, I missed that part." I didn't tell him I was too busy looking for an exit.

We met two waitresses who worked in one of those trolley-car dining places, where we went every night after the gig to eat and talk. They got off work at 2:00 A.M. and would meet one or more of us on the beach, depending on who got lucky and who didn't. On one of these late-night jaunts, one of them asked, "Hey, you want to go and see some

21

magic?" Hell, I thought spending the night swimming naked with two
good-looking girls was magic enough, but I was always ready for something new. So we went back up to the motel and got Ronnie, Packey,
Steve, Duck, and Terry, then climbed into the van and drove down the
beach road until the girls said to stop. We got out and walked down a
long hill to the beach, where the girls told us to start stomping on the
sand and we would see these amazing, magic sparks come flying up. So
what the hell? Off we went down the beach, stomping like madmen looking for the magic. After about thirty minutes of this, we were beginning
to think maybe we were on a snipe hunt. I mean, what did a bunch of
landlocked Tennessee boys know about the sea anyway?

Just as we were about to call it quits, Duck started yelling, "Here it
is, here it is!" We all ran over and started stomping and yelling and dancing, watching hundreds of soft silver blue sparks fly into the air and
disappear in the darkness, like the fading embers of a rocket on the
Fourth of July. We had hit pay dirt. What it turned out to be wasn't magic
at all, but a deposit of phosphorous that I think comes from certain kinds
of fish gills that had washed up on the beach. We had never seen anything
like it, and we quickly stomped the small deposit dry. We were believers
now and started stomping down the dark beach in search of more. After
a while we grew tired of the spark hunting and started walking back up
the beach to where the van was parked. Somewhere along the way we started taking our clothes off and jumping in the ocean. As usual, Packey had
been drinking all night and during our buck-naked frolic, he slipped
away, walked up the hill and got into the van. In his less-than-rational
mind, he thought it would be funny to drive down, headlights on bright,
exposing our bare asses. Since this was four o'clock in the morning on
a deserted strip of beach, I still don't know who he thought would be
watching, but Packey never was one to think that far ahead. So here he
comes roaring down the hill, this silly-looking grin on his face. We all
started yelling, "No, Packey, no!" But it was too late. As soon as he hit
the soft beach he was trapped, sucked up to the hubcaps in the wet sand.

We started digging in earnest. No good. We only dug ourselves in
deeper. We tried putting rocks and sticks under the back wheels, but to
no avail. We were getting nowhere fast. Then the tide came in. We
thought we were getting closer to the ocean; after all, what did we know
about tides and other ocean stuff? When it dawned on us that the ocean
was coming closer to us, panic quickly spread. At this point, we became
aware of an old drunk man sitting on a sand dune behind us. "You're
never going to get it out," he finally said. "I'm the guy who rode the

Packey Axton in Estelle Axton's record shop, 1962.

mule with the rubber tail around the world and I've seen a thousand cars
stuck out here and you're never going to get it out." We believed him.
The waves had started crashing on the front bumper when I put my
clothes on and ran for help. The sun was just peeking above the hori-
zon and, when I reached the outskirts of town, I found a man opening
up a small gas station with a tow truck sitting in the garage. Breathlessly,
I told him of our plight and asked for his help. By the time we got back
to the beach, the sun was full up and shining brightly on these four naked
guys hanging on for dear life to the back bumper of a van that seemed
to be foundering. The truck driver looked down and yelled, "Hey, them
guys is necked! What's going on here?" He seemed to be backing out on
our rescue. I told him there should be a couple of naked girls down there
somewhere and this seemed to pacify him. He ran down with a hook and
a hundred feet of cable and pulled us out. He said, "Boys, two more
minutes and this thing would have ended up in Portugal." Man, were we

relieved. Imagine us calling Mrs. Axton and telling her we had lost the van in the ocean without ever making the first payment on it.

After Myrtle Beach, we played a one-nighter in Jacksonville, and then on to Miami Beach, where we fell in love. The love affair lasted for the next fifteen years, until Miami Beach became too expensive, too crowded, and too mean. We played a huge show at the War Memorial Auditorium and two club dates in Fort Lauderdale and Miami proper.

On the Fourth of July, we were booked for the Big Ape convention. Every year, WAPE radio station threw a big party in the Gator Bowl to celebrate the Fourth. On the show that year, besides us, were Gene Pitney, Charlie Rich, George Jones, Tex Ritter, Faron Young, Del Shannon, Jack Scott, Bobby Vee, the Everly Brothers, and Jerry Lee Lewis. There were 50,000 people there for each of the two shows we were to play that day. One was at two o'clock in the afternoon and, after a big fireworks display, another followed at eight o'clock that evening. The afternoon show went pretty smoothly, except for Jerry Lee's set. Everyone who entered had been given free hotdogs and cokes, and while Jerry Lee was in the middle of his second song, someone threw a weenie on the stage. Jerry Lee made the mistake of picking it up and throwing it back. The stage was set up beneath the goal post at one end of the field, with a hundred yards of people sitting on the grass in front of it. The hotdog had barely left Jerry Lee's hand, when Boom! Hotdogs forever! It looked like a weenie bomb had gone off. The Killer didn't have a chance. He tried to dodge them for a while, but there were way too many. Jerry Lee, bass player J. W. Brown, and drummer Gene Chrisman were covered in mustard and the stage was ankle deep in weenies. It was an awful thing to watch.

The backup band was led by Bobby Vinton, who later had a hit with "Roses Are Red," followed by a string of corny teenage love songs. Up to now, everyone we had met had been like us: trying to do their best to play good music and have a good time. Until we met old Bob.

I was brought up by the old rule that if you can't say anything good about someone, don't say anything at all. But at this point, Bobby Vinton was the worst guy we had met. He was unbelievable, yelling and screaming at everybody. I think today he works in Las Vegas and calls himself the Polish Prince, but to us and everyone else on that show he will always be the Polish Asshole.

ELVIS IN THE MORNING

In Memphis in the late '50s and early '60s there were plenty of Elvis sightings. Everyone had their favorite story of seeing him riding his motorcycle down Lamar Avenue or talking to him at the Pig-n-Whistle or Duke's Drive-In. When I was in high school, Elvis rented a small house at the corner of Kimball and Getwell, in east Memphis. Getwell got its name during World War II, when a giant Veteran's Hospital complex was built there. The name was changed from (believe it or not) Shotwell, in honor of returning GIs who had been wounded at the front. Although this house was only a few blocks from mine, I never knew Elvis was there. But when Elvis moved his family a few blocks away into a new house on Audubon Drive, the whole town knew about it.

In those days, of course, Elvis wasn't idolized the way he was later or is today. He was still accessible to a point, and would meet fans on his front lawn to sign autographs or walk down Main Street with his date. I remember in 1955 he attended the Mid-South Fair and, with a large crowd watching, threw baseballs at milk bottles to win stuffed animals. And you can bet he won. But the thing is, nobody screamed or tried to tear his clothes off. He was one of us. All of these Elvis sightings gathered no importance until years later when he closed himself off from the world.

When Elvis moved to Audubon Drive, he was still only a few blocks away and I often saw him riding around in his German three-wheel Messerschmidt or his pink Cadillac convertible with the top down.

My favorite Elvis experience came in the fall of 1956. I had a morning paper route and got up every morning about four, rode my bike down to pick up my papers, rode back, and walked my route. In those days, the papers had to be on the porch. The days were getting shorter and the sun was coming up about five or five-thirty. I hated getting up every morning, but once I was up and out, I loved it. I guess it was the solitude I really liked. No one was out at that time of morning and it seemed sometimes like I was the only person alive. When I did spot the occasional car or milk truck, it seemed an intrusion and broke the spell. I loved the mornings I didn't see another living being. On one of these cool fall mornings, I was halfway through my route, walking up a long dark hill on Barron Road. I was on the sidewalk and there was a streetlight at the top. Just as I reached the light, I saw a motorcycle coming up the other side of the hill toward me. I stopped to take a look, since I loved motorcycles more than anything. It was a slow-moving Harley, and as it came by me under the street lamp about five feet away, I was

25

eye-to-eye with Elvis and Natalie Wood. They both looked directly at me and I was frozen to the spot. I watched as the red tail lights seemed to float in the darkness down the hill, then up another hill, and vanished. The morning was quiet and still again. This is the kind of stuff that can drive your imagination through the roof. I guess I thought that, since we were the only three out at that time of morning, they might swing back around and stop for a chat under the streetlight. Or maybe ask me to breakfast down at the Gridiron. Maybe even a dip in Elvis's pool before I went to school. I guess when you are fifteen and alone in the dark you go kind of goofy. So off I went, down Barron Road, throwing from the hip, trying to get the paper on the porch.

After the Gator Bowl show, we went home for a few days before heading to Chicago for a week's stand at the Regal Theatre. On our second night at home, I got a call from our singer, Ronnie Stoots. He told me he was at Graceland and for me to go by and pick the rest of the band up and bring them out: Elvis wanted to meet us. Since we knew that Ronnie had been to Graceland a couple of times and was friends with a couple of Elvis's inner circle, we all piled in the van and took off for the gates of Graceland.

It was late, maybe twelve or one o'clock in the morning, but hell, the King wanted to meet us. Since none of us had been to Graceland, we were given explicit directions about where to park: around back in the garage. Back then there was no guard house and the gates were seldom closed. We drove up the long drive and pulled around back, where we found an empty slot in the garage. It wasn't really a garage, but a long open-ended pavilion with room for about ten cars. We parked, got out, and walked through the garage, which opened on to the backyard.

The lights had been on in the front, bright spotlights that lit up the big pillars in the circular driveway, but the back was pitch black. We were about halfway between the garage and the back door when it seemed like the whole world exploded. From everywhere, multicolored balls of fire came swooshing at us. We were paralyzed. We huddled together in the middle of the yard until the deluge was over. The back floodlights came on, revealing dark figures stumbling out of the bushes, laughing their asses off. We had been suckered.

Fireworks were illegal in Memphis, so Elvis had driven over to Arkansas, bought an entire firework stand, loaded them on a truck, and brought it back, a small portion of which he'd set off in our honor.

Although it was four days after the Fourth, old E was still celebrating. Since we had no choice but to be good sports about the whole thing, we were invited to stay the night, shooting all the fireworks we could light. Altogether, there must have been fifteen or twenty of us, and we spent the night shooting off these giant rockets and choosing up sides for Roman candle fights. Elvis wore his motorcycle jacket and helmet, with a scarf wrapped around his neck to protect him from the fiery little missiles. The rest of us were on our own. I tried my best to shield my eyes with one hand while I aimed and fired with the other. This went on until the sun came up.

Elvis announced as everyone was leaving, "If anyone got any burns on their shirt" (which just about everyone did) "go down to Lansky's and get a new one and tell him I sent you." Although I did have a couple of holes in my shirt, I never did go get my free one. To this day I wish I had. It would have been the first time I walked out of Lansky's without spending any money.

After that, any time we were home the same time as Elvis, we went to Graceland or to one of his all-night parties at the Memphian Theater, Rainbow Skating Rink, or the Memphis Fairgrounds. But looking back on those days it seems to me there were two Elvises. The first was the one I saw, hanging out, playing pranks, laughing, and having fun. The other Elvis came later. The one no one saw. The one who had all the trouble.

ON THE ROAD

THE REGAL

We left for Chicago early Sunday morning, pulling in well after sunset. There were no interstates to speak of in 1961, which made traveling by car a long and tedious job. We took turns driving, all except Terry. We did not let Terry Johnson drive under any circumstances. We drove around for a while looking for a hotel, finally settling on the Blackhawk for no other reason than we liked the name. The Regal Theatre was in the heart of south Chicago. There were no white people. I don't mean just a few or not very many, I mean *NONE*. We stuck out like whores in church. It was an old theater, part of what the R&B acts called the Chitlin' Circuit, a group of theaters throughout the midwest and northeast where they played week-long engagements. Most of these theaters showed a movie, followed by a music concert with as many as fifteen acts, backed by a large orchestra. They usually got started at about one in the afternoon. After the movie and the show, the audience left and another one was admitted. This went on for three shows during the week and four on weekends.

There were nine acts on the show that week, other than us, acts like Wade Flemons, the Simms Twins, Little Caesar and the Romans, and the headliner, LaVern Baker. I had grown up listening to her records, like "Tweedle Dee" and "Jim Dandy." Because she was the headliner, she performed last and, instead of doing only two songs like everybody else, she could sing as many as she wanted. She was the star, a fact everyone backstage was made aware of. Not that she wasn't nice, she just carried herself like someone who was used to getting her way. I think we were kind of scared of her, but we couldn't wait to see her perform.

That week in Chicago on the top R&B station, our record "Last Night" was Number 1, and the flipside, "The Night Before," was Number 2, which meant that we would go on next-to-last and do four songs. We had to be at the theater at twelve o'clock every day, so sleeping late was out of the question. Since there were eight of us, we got the largest dressing room. Actually, we had two rooms with windows overlooking the alley that ran behind the building. Large windows opened onto a fire escape, where we could sit at night in the cool air. There were cots to

29

take naps, and we quickly found out there was much more entertainment backstage than out front.

The twenty-two-piece orchestra was led by Red Saunders. Red was
a drummer, but had two other drummers in the band: the great Larry
"Wild" Rice and Red Saunders, Jr. This was one kicking band filled with
a Who's Who of Chicago jazz players. Charles "Chippy" Champion was
the bassist. He had played with everybody and went on to play with Count
Basie a few years later. We walked around backstage that first day in a
trance. We never imagined in our wildest dreams that anything like this
went on anywhere. The orchestra's dressing rooms were downstairs in
the basement where, between shows, high-stakes poker games took place.
The lead saxophonist was the sheriff of Cook County and the whole band
had been deputized, which meant they all carried guns. What fascinated
me most was the fact that you could buy anything backstage at the Regal
Theatre in Chicago, and I do mean *anything*. That first day a lot of people
dropped by to see what was happening and to say hello, people like
Phillip Upchurch, Jerry Butler, the Impressions, and Sam Cook. Mix
all this together with eight teenage white boys and a Tarzan movie out
front. We were in heaven.

The first day we were in our dressing rooms after the movie while
the MC warmed up the audience for the concert. There had been
rehearsals the day before, which we had not attended since we were the
only self-contained group in the show. We had been told we would go
on after Wade Flemons and before LaVern Baker and that was it. The
drums, amps, and piano were on risers with wheels so they could be easily
and quickly rolled into place. The door was closed and we were just
sitting around waiting for things to get started when that twenty-two-
piece band kicked off with an instrumental. The walls shook and the
chairs we were sitting on started to vibrate. We jumped up and ran out
onto the landing two floors above the stage. Up to this point I had never
seen a band this big. I had seen large bands on TV, but nothing to
compare to these guys. They were fantastic. I thought we might hold our
own with the other acts on the show, but who would want to hear our
measly three-piece horn section after listening to this band for an hour?
Backstage may have been bedlam before, but the minute the show started,
it ran like a well-oiled machine. As soon as an act was through, a curtain came down in front of the orchestra. Then two curtains came together in front of that one, leaving about eight or nine feet in between
for the next act to get in place. It ran like clockwork, and then it was our
turn. Wade Flemons came off and wished us good luck. The stage hands

rolled our instruments into place and Duck and Steve plugged in while Packey, Wayne, and I did some last-minute tuning and we were on. We still were without publicity photos and you could see the shock on some of the audience's faces as the curtains separated, revealing seven skinny white boys.

We started that first show with a semi-jazz tune called "Sack-o-Woe" by Cannonball Adderly, written by his brother Nat. About halfway through the song you could see the expressions on people's faces change. They slowly went from suspicion to approval. They were getting in to it and so were we. You could feel things loosen up.

Our second song was "The Night Before," which we played with growing confidence. For the third song we brought Ronnie on to sing "Ebbtide." The band did a somewhat different version of this song that really highlighted Ronnie's voice, and they loved him. The Regal had a strict rule about dancing. You could stand in front of your seat and dance in place, but no one was allowed in the aisles. Our last song, of course, was "Last Night" and as soon as the horn swell started, you could see them coming up out of their seats, and on the first downbeat the place went crazy. People poured into the aisles. The Pony was the dance of the day and everyone was doing it; in the aisles, on their seats, people were dancing everywhere.

We had never seen an audience react to our music like this, but the biggest surprise came near the end of the song, where there's a two-bar break while I lean in to the mike and say, "Oh, yeah!" After this, Terry hits a single snare shot, sending us back into the last two verses. Only this time, there were four snare shots. The curtain in front of the orchestra had remained down during our set so they could take a little break but, much to our surprise, they had returned. As the curtain slowly rose, they all played along. It made the hair on the back of my neck stand up, and when the song ended, the place was almost out of control. People were rushing down the aisle toward the stage as the curtain closed. Members of the band and some of the other acts were waiting for us as we left the stage. They were hugging us, slapping us on the back, shaking hands, and telling us how much they enjoyed our set. We couldn't believe it: Had we died and gone to heaven? I think what most entertainers strive for is the acceptance of other entertainers and, in our case, this would be all the approval we ever needed.

Then it was time for LaVern Baker and she came on sounding great, singing her old hits. But during the last part of her act, I think she tried to show a different side of her singing ability and did a lot of songs with more of a cabaret feel: legit songs that the mostly younger audience didn't pick up on. She was not called back for an encore. The other two shows that day went even better. Everyone settled in and grew more confident as the orchestra grew more familiar with the charts. After the last show that night, we were happy, tired, and ready for some sleep, but Chippy Champion and Larry Rice had other plans. After we had packed everything away, they came over. "You guys ready to see south Chicago?" For the next week, we spent our nights and early mornings prowling the streets and alleyways of that part of town. We went to clubs, cabarets, and speakeasies with Chippy and Larry as our guides and protectors. I think they enjoyed showing us naive Tennessee boys the other side of Chicago, and we sure as hell enjoyed seeing it.

That first night they took us to a speakeasy behind a funeral parlor. As we entered, we were frisked for weapons and, although we knew that both Chippy and Larry were packing, nobody ever mentioned it. I mean, why go through the motions of a thorough patdown and never ask the guys to check their guns? It led us to believe that Larry and Chippy were more connected than we thought. When we left, we took the train to Rice Street, where we sat in a small club and listened to Sonny Stitt, Gene Ammons, Dexter Gordon, Benny Green, and Brother Jack McDuff in the greatest jam session any of us had ever heard.

The second day, we arrived at the theater to find there had been a change in the schedule. We would now go on last in LaVern Baker's place, and she would take our spot. She was mad; she was real bad mad. Her dressing room was next to ours and we could hear the commotion when she got the news. I know now how embarrassed she must have been to be replaced as the headliner by one-hit wonders like us. All we wanted to do was play and were willing to keep things like they were. Hell, we were just glad to be there. We knew we were a long way from being the professional that LaVern Baker was, but the powers-that-be stood by their decision and that's the way the show ran for the rest of the week.

The headliner spot gave us time to stretch out, mixing our instrumentals with Ronnie's superb vocals. I even sang my rendition of Bobby Marchans's "There's Something on Your Mind." I had my own version of the recitation, a comedy version that lead into the Isley Brothers' "Shout." But no matter what song we did, the biggest reaction was always to "Last Night." The ushers and security people had finally given up on trying to keep the audience from dancing in the aisles. We couldn't wait to hear Red Saunders and that big band joining us on the last two verses. By the end of the week we had stretched it to ten verses just so we

32

could play along with that great band. We hated for that last show to be over. I don't think we were ready for the way people treated us—not only the audience, but the people backstage, who were kind and helpful. That week was a real eye-opener for all of us and a school we couldn't have paid for.

The only hitch all week had been the LaVern Baker episode. She didn't hang out much and stayed in her dressing room except when she was on stage. Wade Flemons became a good friend that week and, right before the last show, he came to our dressing room. "Guys, if you want to make LaVern happy, go out and buy her a dozen roses and a bottle of champagne," which is exactly what we did. We gathered around her door, all eight of us. When she opened the door, Wayne told her what an honor it had been to appear with her that week. We handed her the flowers and champagne, which one of the stagehands had put in a bucket of ice. We stood there looking at each other for a few seconds and then she started to cry—I mean huge tears. That night at a farewell party at one of south Chicago's finest speakeasies, she stood up, raised her glass, and made a toast, "To The Mar-Keys, the best band in the land!" No matter where we played after that, we always compared it to the week we spent at the Regal Theatre; to this day, nothing has ever come close.

❋　　❋　　❋

33

We came back to Memphis to record and I got to play on my first million-seller, William Bell's "You Don't Miss Your Water." William had been one of the Del Rios, whom we had heard perform a few years before at the Plantation Inn. He was also a gentlemen in every sense of the word: very soft-spoken, polite, someone we enjoyed working with. Stax was beginning to change. It was becoming a thriving business instead of our rehearsal hall and hangout. This was inevitable, I guess, but I hated to see those days go.

THE SWAMP

Southern Louisiana was a deep, dark, low-down kind of place with an eerie feel about it. I think if we had our choice, we would have turned around and gone home, but we had four days booked there and binding contracts that couldn't be broken. That week we were to play Lafayette, New Iberia, Crowley, and Beau Bridge, four small towns within a radius of 100 miles. Since Lafayette was centrally located, we rented motel rooms and worked out of there. The gigs in Lafayette and Beau

Don Nix accompanies Billy Bland at the
Royal Peacock Social Club, Atlanta, 1961.

Bridge went smoothly, but Crowley and New Iberia were another story.
Crowley was a depressed area and the club we played held about 200
people, but as the night wore on, the crowd grew to twice that size. Everybody called each other "Coon Ass" or "Field Nigger," and the names
they had for us were a little less flattering. I wanted to get a bus back to
Memphis, but some false sense of security made me stay.

I've always been one of those people who leave any situation that
feels the slightest bit strange. Even to this day, I'm gone in a flash if I
walk into a club, studio, or anywhere that feels even a little bit uncomfortable. The club in Crowley was quickly becoming more uncomfortable than anybody wanted to admit. To top matters off, there were two
white detectives who stood behind us all night. I mean if we were in our
dressing room, they were right there. Even on stage they stood behind
us and watched us like hawks. They said things like, "We know you guys
have got some drugs, and we're going to find them." So there we were,
stuck between a rock and a hard place: an incredibly unruly crowd in
front of us and the Louisiana State Police behind.

The crowd had now swelled to over 450 and they seemed to be
building toward something, something that wasn't going to be very

pleasant. Sure enough, a fight broke out in the back of the club. Not one of those fights where a few punches are thrown and the bouncers break it up. This one the bouncers actually started, and it was a doozy. Like rolling thunder, it proceeded toward the front, sucking up chairs, tables, and people as it came. We did not wait for the management to tell us to leave. I had left my horn case right behind the bandstand, and as I was packing my horn away, I noticed this big black guy standing over me. I had just bought a metal mouthpiece for my baritone, and as I was taking it off the horn to put it in the case he says, "I've always wanted me a mouthpiece like that," but the way he said it was like, "If you don't give me that mouthpiece I'm gonna kill you!" By now I didn't give a shit. I just wanted to get out of there. So I stood up, handed him the mouthpiece, and said, "Now you've got one, asshole. I hope you choke on it." He just stood there kind of shocked, like I had handed him a grenade or something. This gave me time to grab my horn and go out an open window.

By now, the fight had spread to the parking lot and people were fighting everywhere. It was like running an obstacle course, but eventually everyone made it to the truck, and we were off, heading west on Highway 90 to Lafayette. The road was like a straight, narrow black ribbon, cutting through the south Louisiana countryside. As we put more miles between us and the club, we began to relax. Packey was driving and we had the windows rolled down, enjoying the cool Louisiana evening. There was no moon, no traffic, and the night was as black as the angel of death. The country was low flatland and you could see forever. There was only one other car on the road besides us and we could see its tail-lights about a mile ahead. Suddenly, the brake lights appeared on the car in front of us. We saw to our left the revolving light of an approaching freight train, and the car in front was slowing down to see if he could beat it to the crossing. Evidently he thought he could, because the brake lights went off and the car seemed to pick up speed.

We were still a quarter of a mile behind, so Packey started eyeing the train to see if *we* could beat it too—a bad idea. I was sitting in the front between Packey and Steve, and I was starting to have my doubts about whether we were going to beat that train. I told Packey, "Maybe we should stop. We've got all night. We've just gotten out of one bad situation, let's not get ourselves into another." Packey looked at me and I could see his face from the lights of the dash, and I could tell by that mischievous, drunken grin of his that he was going to beat this train if it harelipped the Maid of Cotton.

We started picking up speed and everybody's looking to our left, watching the approaching train. About this time, it occurred to me that maybe this crossing had a signal gate, so I directed my gaze back to the front to have a look. I didn't see a signal gate, but what I did see was a tan-over-brown '58 Oldsmobile sitting dead ahead of us. The driver had changed his mind and decided to stop for the train. I didn't have time to yell a warning and we hit the rear of the Olds full out. Packey never came close to the brake and the impact knocked the Olds across the tracks right in front of the train. It stopped us dead, leaving just enough room for the train to pass between us. It was then that we discovered it wasn't a freight, but a fast-moving passenger train going ninety miles an hour. It was no more than three feet in front of us and the noise was deafening. Our headlights, which were miraculously still on, reflected off the silver passenger cars, almost blinding us. We sat there, petrified like stick men, until the train had passed. Later, I wondered about what the engineer must have thought as he passed between these two cars out on the dark Louisiana flats. I figured he probably had chest pains all the way to Chicago. The train was gone in a flash, leaving us sitting there in a terrified trance.

What our headlights shone on then was almost unbelievable. There had been ten occupants in the car, and now they were out and running. All four doors were open and people were everywhere. There were a few in the rice fields to our right, knee deep in water. A few in the ditch on our left, wandering around aimlessly. There was even one guy in the middle of the highway on his knees praying, "Oh thank you Lord. Thank you Jesus." They had one thing in common: They were all drunker than Packey ever thought about being. It took us a good ten minutes to round everybody up and we were relieved to find that no one was injured. I walked over to where Packey was talking to the other driver, who was begging him not to call the police because he was drunk. Packey quickly agreed. It was amazing how little damage our van had sustained while leaving the rear of the Olds a complete wreck. While no cops were called that night, we still felt bad about the damage to the other guy's car, so we pooled our money and gave it to him to make repairs. It was incredible that no one out of the eighteen people in the two vehicles was hurt. Despite the damage to the Olds, it was still roadworthy, so everybody jumped in and they disappeared into the night, leaving us standing on the highway, wondering what had happened. One thing we did know for sure: Packey had lost his driving privileges forever.

When we arrived back at our motel rooms, we discovered the cops had kept their promise about busting us for drugs because all our rooms had been searched. Since none of us had gotten into drugs yet, they had wasted their time. We would have probably left for home right then if it hadn't been for the fact that we hadn't been paid for any of the gigs we had already played. Can you see a pattern forming here? I wish we had. The last gig was to take place in New Iberia, the next afternoon at two o'clock. After the harrowing experiences of the previous night, none of us slept very well except Packey, who had passed out in the van before we got back to the motel.

We got up about noon and checked out because we had no intentions of staying in that God-forsaken place any longer than necessary. After driving to New Iberia, we wandered around looking for the club, but what we found wasn't really a club at all, but a condemned building in the middle of a marsh—kind of like the nightclub in the movie *The Color Purple*. It had a low ceiling held up by four walls and two rows of four-by-fours down the middle. The tables and chairs were from mixed-

Admission card for the Dude Ranch Nite Club, 1961.

and-matched kitchen and dinette sets, which made the whole place re-
semble some macabre flea market. The only good thing about it was a
large bandstand at one end of the building and the fact that they were
selling decent barbecue ribs and beer by the quart. Also, I liked the idea
of playing this gig in the afternoon, since statistics show that most mur-
ders take place at night. This was not someplace you'd want to be after
dark.

It was Sunday and most of the all-black audience came directly from
church, chowing down on racks of ribs and white bread and washing it
all down with cold beer or harder spirits they carried in their coat pockets and purses. By the time we set up and started playing, the place was
packed with folks eating and talking. They listened to the music and ap-
plauded politely after each song, but as the afternoon wore on and the
beer and the booze started taking effect, things really started jumping.
After the first set, I went to the restroom, which beat anything I'd ever
seen as far as toilets go. It was a big room built on the back of the place
with a six-inch-wide hole in the floor. This place made Neil's Hideaway
look like the Russian Tea Room. I was about sixth in line, hoping like
hell the hole didn't fill up before I got to it. Don't get me wrong, we
didn't think we were too good for this place, or any place like it. We had
been playing roadhouses, joints, and dives since we started, but now we
had a record in the charts and if we didn't make it now, we never would.
So I'm standing there, trying to hit this hole and not piss on my shoe,
when a drunk guy walks up and says, "Hey man, let me hold a dolla'."
Damn, I loved show business.

By the last set, people were getting really drunk and a lot of them
were dancing, although there was no dance floor. They danced where
they stood, on the bandstand, even on tables, but were much better be-
haved than the crowds of the past few evenings. There was a uniformed
security guard on duty, but he mostly walked up and down the center
aisle of the building or stood about twenty feet in front of the bandstand, listening to the music. He was a big guy and he stood there lean-
ing on one of the four-by-fours, his right hand holding a well-used billy club and his left hand propped on his hip, about six inches above the
gun he carried. He had his back to the door, so he didn't see this guy
come dancing in. His clothes fit him real loose, and as he came high-
stepping down the middle of the building, he looked like a day's wash
hanging on the line. He could really dance though, in a kind of a roaring '20s, bebop style. He had this big gold-tooth grin on his face, and
you could tell he had come to party. He was looking at us the whole time,

but when he got just behind the security guard he spotted the officer's Smith & Wesson protruding from the holster. He stopped in a freeze pose, sort of like John Travolta in *Saturday Night Fever,* his gaze locked on the gun. We saw it coming, but there was nothing we could do. He grabbed the gun, fired two shots into the ceiling, put it back in the holster, turned around, and started dancing back toward the door before the cop ever turned around. When he did, he came down with the billy club across the back of the dancing man's head, folding him like a rubber crutch, and leaving him lying in the middle of the place like a pile of dirty laundry. All this happened so fast, we didn't miss a beat, but we had seen enough. We packed up, piled in, and headed for home. Of course, the promoter skipped out with the money, but we did get paid a year later after promising we'd play a return engagement when he paid for the first one. We were surprised when he did send the money, but of course we cashed the check and stayed at home.

After Chicago we played Miami again, and some one-nighters in northern Florida and Georgia, with a two-night stand at the famous Royal Peacock Club on Auburn Street in Atlanta. The Peacock was an all-black supper club in those days, and we appeared with Titus Turner and Billy Bland, who had had a big record, "Let the Little Girl Dance." In most of these places we had had a great time, up until the Louisiana trip. However, I did see one thing that really shook me up.

While driving through southern Georgia on a stifling hot August afternoon, we came upon a chain gang—a *real* chain gang, with black-and-white striped uniforms and everyone connected by heavy ankle chains. The guards wore riding britches with shining tight knee-high boots, Smokey the Bear hats, and mirrored sunglasses. They were armed with twelve-gauge pump guns and it didn't look like they had much give to 'em. The convicts were laying asphalt and we had to slow down to get around them. We passed within five feet of those guys grunting, sweating, and humping asphalt that was so hot, thick smoke obliterated the whole scene at times. We sat there watching this bizarre play and were all probably thinking the same thing: "Be good. Be gooder than good. 'Cause nothin' is worth ending up in a line with these poor souls."

Although we were young and naive, not one of us thought this would last forever and it made no difference that we sometimes made more in one night than we had in a month, 'cause we spent it all anyway, every last cent. That is, except Steve Cropper, who was the only one with a bank account. If any of the rest of us were suspected of squirreling a few bucks away, the others were on him, urging, "Spend it. Spend it all." In Miami we had attempted to stay at the prestigious and expensive Fountainbleu Hotel, but were denied rooms because of our less-than-fashionable attire. Undaunted, we went down the street to the Moulin Rouge, where our rooms cost us more than we made that night; we knew we would never have another chance like this again and good times didn't come for free.

We came in from Louisiana dog-tired, broke again, and with a slightly different outlook toward the road. We'd been having a good time, but it was beginning to take its toll. The distance between gigs seemed to get longer every trip and travel with eight people could be frustrating, no matter how close friends we were. Also, PA systems were almost nonexistent in most places, and when there was one, it usually turned out to be a Guy Lombardo model that had seen better days. A lot of nights we had to run a vocal mike through either the bass or guitar amp. The seeds of rock 'n' roll were still being sown and sometimes it was hard to keep on farming. By the fall of '61, Steve Cropper had seen enough. At the end of a long hot summer that started what seemed like years ago, Steve left and Charlie Freeman came back aboard on guitar.

Steve wanted to stay at Stax and work in the record shop or studio and try his hand at producing and writing. I think Crop was always the reasonable one among us, the safe one, and this decision turned out to be a good one. Charlie had turned into a connoisseur of jazz since his days playing the Gulf Coast with the Joe Lee Orchestra, and I think his playing suffered from this. Steve is probably the best rhythm guitar player I've ever heard, with that big, deep, full sound that really makes a rhythm section cook. Charlie was just the opposite at that time, playing with a thin, sparse sound that he thought passed for jazz. He had changed in the past six months and was drinking just as much as Packey. By this time, I knew my days were numbered as well. We still weren't playing on most of our records, which were mostly recorded by other musicians while we were on the road. After the third single without a hit, I told one of the guys, "If you're gonna cut our records for us, at least cut some hits—we're dying out there." They weren't amused. I didn't realize that in a year this would all be a memory anyway.

The only photo taken of the Mar-Keys with both Steve Cropper and Charlie Freeman present; Memphis, 1961. <u>Left</u> <u>to</u> <u>right</u>, <u>back</u> <u>row</u>: Duck Dunn, Packey Axton, Don Nix, Charlie Freeman; <u>front</u> <u>row</u>: Terry Johnson, Wayne Jackson, Steve Cropper.

THE HURRICANE

Our first trip with Charlie was to Liberty, Texas, for a weekend club gig. It was also the start of the hurricane season, and there was a big one brewing in the Gulf of Mexico. We left on a Thursday night to get there in time for a Friday evening gig. We liked to drive at night since there was less traffic on the road, but by the next morning, as we were heading south on Highway 59 from Lufkin, we saw this endless line of cars coming north in a great exodus of the lowlands. It seemed kind of exciting at the time 'cause we knew by radio reports that the hurricane was serious and would probably make landfall somewhere between Port Arthur and Galveston. If you check your map, you'll find Liberty just inland right between those two towns. But what the hell, we had the foolishness of youth on our side and we had never seen a hurricane. We had heard of hurricane parties and wanted in on the action.

The farther south we drove, the less traffic we saw and finally we were the only ones on the road. We told each other we had to show up, otherwise we could be sued by the club owner since we had a signed contract. (The truth was, of course, we wanted to be in a hurricane real bad.) We pulled into Liberty Friday afternoon, just as the first few raindrops started to fall. We found a ghost town with absolutely no other living soul in sight; besides the traffic light swinging in the ever-increasing breeze, we were the only thing moving. We drove around looking for the club, which of course was locked tight and boarded up, but we figured we had met our contractual agreement and went looking for the closest hurricane party.

Of course, we didn't find one, so we decided to have one ourselves at the nearest motel. The owner was just locking up; when we asked if he had any vacant rooms, he looked at us like we were mad. He said, "They're all vacant. You can have as many as you want, as long as you pay in advance." We watched as he got in his car and headed north, shaking his head like he had just left a bunch of escapees from the county home for the feebleminded. The White Heron motel was one of those '50s low-flat, one-story places, with rooms built out on either side of an office in the center. As the storm picked up speed, we drove around looking for a place to eat, but finding none, settled on some candy bars we found in the vending machine outside a service station.

We drove back to the motel and settled into the four rooms we had rented to wait for the hurricane. We didn't have to wait long. Around two o'clock in the morning, we lost our electricity and sat around in the dark listening to a battery-operated radio we always carried. Everyone congregated in the room Duck and I were sharing until daybreak, when everybody went to their own rooms for some shut-eye. After the long drive from Memphis, I fell asleep with my clothes on and slept until about ten o'clock Saturday morning. Although it was mid-morning, it was still dark. There was a low howling sound that gave me goosebumps. I had never heard the wind howl like that, and it was so strong it was blowing leaves and grass under our door and the floor was ankle-deep in foliage. I looked out the small window in our door just in time to see a trailer from the trailer park behind us go tumbling end over end across the highway. Maybe this wasn't going to be as much fun as we thought. The rain was blowing sideways and was so heavy we could barely see the van parked just outside the door. Duck woke up in a panic. He couldn't swim and had always been afraid of water. With all the wind and rain, he figured, the ocean was going to come and drown us. The rest of us weren't so sure he was wrong.

As the afternoon wore on, the storm grew in intensity, and just when we were sure it couldn't get any worse, it got worse. The batteries were getting low on our radio, and one of the last weather forecasts we heard told us of numerous tornadoes being spawned by the hurricane. We were southern boys and what we didn't know about hurricanes, we made up for in tornado knowledge. Duck was beside himself and took a mattress off one of the beds, pinning himself in a corner. No one had said anything about tornadoes up until now, and we all sat huddled in one room again, wondering how we had let this happen. About two o'clock Sunday morning things got very still and we ventured outside the room for the first time in hours. We realized this was the eye of the storm passing over; we were in a vacuum, and it's one of the strangest feelings I've ever had. The stillness lasted for about forty minutes before the storm resumed its unbelievable onslaught. We sat in the one room all night and until noon the next day before the wind subsided and the rain slowed to a drizzle.

When we did get out in the van driving around, looking for something to eat, we realized that, because of its low profile, our motel was one of the few buildings left standing in that part of town. Once again, we proved that God watches over those who are too dumb to watch out for themselves. We drove around dodging downed power lines, trees, and other debris trying to find our way out of town. We passed a vacant lot where the club we were to have played once stood. We drove to Galveston, where we were some of the first to see the awful destruction the hurricane and tornadoes had wreaked on that beautiful city. We were so broke we didn't even have the money to get back home, and called our booking agent for some help. He kept $1300 of our money in escrow in case of emergencies, so we lied to him and told him our van had broken down and we needed the money to put a new motor in it.

Most of us didn't even have money for food. I remember Wayne Jackson hocked his watch for two ham sandwiches, then sat in front of us and ate them (something I've never quite forgiven him for). We had called from the highway in the first phone booth we found operational and had the agent send the money to the Western Union office in Del Rio, Texas. Part of my brief stint in the army was spent at Fort Sam Houston in San Antonio, and I spent weekends across the border in Mexico. I had always told the guys what a wild time you could have there on just a little money, and now they wanted to see it for themselves. We justified this trip by telling ourselves that we deserved a little R&R after what we had been through the past weekend, and as soon as we picked up the money we disappeared across the border for four days. I won't go into great detail about our time in Mexico, except to say it didn't involve any donkeys or goats and we promised ourselves to return as soon

The Mar-Keys, Birmingham, 1962.

as we could. We got back home tired and broke again, but with a pretty good adventure locked in our memories forever.

THE KILLER DOES IT AGAIN

After most of our trips, we stayed home for just a few days. These days I spent at the studio or at Ray Brown's office waiting for news of the next gig. One morning I arrived at Ray's to find him in his office, his head on the desk, crying. I thought maybe he had lost a member of his family and rushed around behind him, placing my hand on his shoulder and doing my best to comfort him. He finally looked at me between sobs and said something about killing Jerry Lee Lewis. Since Jerry Lee's career had taken a nosedive after he married his thirteen-year-old cousin, Ray had been booking him for nickel-and-dime gigs around the South and Midwest. Ray had always thought that if he could just book Jerry Lee into one of the big hotels in Las Vegas it would be a goldmine for both of them. After all, it was the Killer's name that had been tarnished, not his singing or playing, and he was still the best act in rock 'n' roll.

After years of trying, Ray had finally booked Jerry for a two-week stand in the dinner club of one of the big hotels. Eventually I got Ray calmed down enough to tell me what had happened. It seemed that Jerry Lee had opened the night before. There was trouble right away when the waiters started serving dinner in the middle of the Killer's set. He became enraged and started cursing them as they passed in front of the stage with trays piled high with food and drink. One of the waiters got tired of being harassed and gave Jerry Lee the finger as he came by. Jerry went crazy, and taking the microphone stand with both hands, he swung the base, catching the guy under the chin, lifting him off his feet, and scattering broccoli, prime rib, and fruit cocktail over the front four tables.

Ray started bawling again, and I had to do some more comforting to get him to finish telling me what had happened. I said "That doesn't sound so bad, at least he didn't kill the guy." Ray raised his head, tears running down his face, saying, "No, that's not all, it gets a lot worse."

Jerry Lee was in the middle of his last song when he spotted some people standing in the back of the room clapping along with his pumping piano. They were black people and Jerry Lee didn't like it at all. He grabbed the mike, stood up and yelled, "Tell them niggers to sit down back there!" The audience turned to see who the Killer was talking about. The "niggers" turned out to be Sammy Davis, Jr., and Bill Cosby, who had come up to see Jerry and wish him luck. The Killer had shot himself in the foot again. He was fired on the spot and sent packing to play VFW halls and roadhouses for the rest of his life. I left Ray with his head on his desk envisioning all that money flying out the window. A few years later, Ray's kidneys quit on him and he died. I've always thought that night in Vegas played a big part in Ray Brown's death.

45

I WAS ASKED TO LEAVE GRACELAND

Charlie Freeman had just rejoined the band, and had not yet been to Graceland. So when Jim Kingsley and Richard Davis, two of Elvis's inner circle and friends of ours called to invite us to the Memphian Theatre for some all-night movies, we went by and picked up Charlie. It was after midnight and Charlie came out carrying his guitar case. He was hoping to jam with Elvis, Scottie, Bill, and the guys. During our frequent visits to Graceland, we had seen no jam sessions except for Elvis singing hymns and playing the big Hammond organ in the living room. We told Charlie this, but since he had been drinking all night, he had his mind made up and he was ready to jam.

There were usually about twenty to twenty-five people at the Memphian when Elvis rented the theater. After the last movie, we caravaned out to Graceland, where we stayed up until Elvis went to bed after the sun came up. That night, after the last movie, we drove out to Graceland and waited in the circle driveway in front of the house while Elvis parked around back. He came around with his guys and Anita Wood and stood on the steps overlooking the fifteen or twenty people gathered before him and announced there would be no party this morning. He was tired and wanted to get some sleep, since there was going to be a big touch football game the next afternoon in a field behind the house.

As everyone was leaving, Elvis yelled at someone near us, "Hey, you gonna play tomorrow?" Charlie saw his chance. He had been standing there waiting patiently, holding that big ol' guitar case of his. "Hell, let's play tonight!" he yelled. One of ol' E's guys looked down at Charlie, spotted the guitar in his hand, and said, "He's not talking about music, he's talking about football." Charlie couldn't believe his ears. "Fuck a bunch of football!" he screamed. "I'm here to jam!" Everybody kind of froze in place for a second and then, like a whirlwind, two or three of Elvis's guys had Charlie by the neck, rushed him down the long drive-way, and put him on the street, guitar and all.

Charlie found out the hard way that you didn't talk to the King like that, especially when he was preparing for a big game. We were a little embarrassed, not only for Charlie, but for the fact we had driven all the way out there at four o'clock in the morning only to be sent home like a bunch of naughty children. That was my last visit to Graceland, although I did go to the midnight movie sessions and a couple of the all-night fairgrounds parties. I had begun to feel like one of those pathetic souls who did nothing but eat, sleep, and dream Elvis. Some of those people spent their whole lives doing nothing but trying to please the King. The sad part about it is there are still people like that to this day, devoting a good part of their lives to a guy who's left the building for good.

ON THE ROAD AGAIN

One of my favorite records of 1961 was *Tossin' and Turnin'* by Bobby Lewis, so I was happy when Ray called to tell us we were booked for a fourteen-day tour of the Southwest with him. Bobby was from the Northeast and didn't know what to think about running around Texas and Oklahoma with a bunch of southern white boys. Remember, this is still 1961, and it was not at all cool for blacks and whites to be traveling together in that part of the world. After the first gig in Dallas, we quickly became close friends with Bobby. On stage we were family, but off stage was another matter. After each gig, Bobby disappeared and we didn't see him until just before showtime at the next town. We played mostly large clubs, some black and some white. I think it made Bobby really nervous to be in that part of the country. When the last show was over in Houston, he immediately headed North while we headed South, back to Mexico.

After a couple of days of bordertown fun (which this time, according to Smoochie, did include a small donkey this time), we headed north back across the border to call Ray for some more money. He was in a panic. "Where the hell have you guys been?" he screamed over the phone. "I've been trying to reach you for three days. I've got you booked on a big tour and it starts tomorrow night and you've got to make it!" "Where does this tour start?" I asked. All at once, Ray's voice was little more than a whisper. "Speak up Ray, I can't hear you." "Norfolk, Virginia," he replied in a louder yet meeker tone. "How far is that, Ray?" I asked, without really wanting to know. His voice was gaining authority now. "I think it's about a thousand miles, but if you leave right now you can make it in plenty of time." It was midday, which meant we had less than thirty hours before showtime. We had been up for two days, and it's a miracle no one fell asleep on the way to Virginia.

Ray Brown was wrong about the distance. It was more like fifteen hundred miles, and we stopped briefly in Memphis to call him up and cuss him. We rolled up behind the Norfolk auditorium one hour before the show, and I still don't know how we made it. There was only one small problem. Lloyd Price and his big band were supposed to back the other acts on the show, but Lloyd had been arrested and was in jail in South Carolina, and guess who the promoter wanted to take his place? They were all in our dressing room explaining how, if we didn't back the show there wouldn't be a show, and we were trying to explain that we didn't even know who was on the show, much less know their songs. Finally the promoter stood up and told us matter-of-factly, "No show, no pay!" Well, that did it. "Who's on the show?" we asked. There were ten other acts besides us, including Chuck Berry, Freddy Cannon, Baby Washington, the Cleftones, the Jarmels, the Drifters, Jerry Butler, and the one and only Bobby Lewis, whom we had just left three days before.

Somehow we made it through that first show without fainting on stage. I grabbed a tambourine and kept a pretty steady backbeat through the whole thing. The first time we ever saw most of the acts was when they walked on stage in front of us. The Drifters' guitar player played with us and carried most of the rhythm, and I don't think most of the three or four thousand people in the audience knew the difference. That is, until Bobby Lewis came on. We had been playing his songs for the past two weeks and had them down pat. He was the hit of the night and was even called back for two encores. The other acts didn't know that we had just finished a tour with Bobby, and I'm sure they wondered how we could play so well behind him and so poorly behind them. We had to back the show for the next two dates, but we did have some time to re-hearse with each act and things went a little smoother. Still, we were re-lieved when Lloyd Price got out of jail and he and his fifteen-piece band rejoined the tour.

The next week we took a few days' rest and rejoined the tour on De-cember 3 in Knoxville. The Ike and Tina Turner Review had replaced Lloyd Price as backing band and headliner. Another new addition was Lee Dorsey, who had been traveling with the review since his hit "Ya Ya" and was drinking pretty heavily in those days. Most nights, Ike intro-duced him and then placed a chair in front of the mike and Lee was helped to the stage and sat while singing four or five songs. His only stage accessory was a rubber bow tie with an elastic band, which he pulled out of his pocket and stretched over his head just before going on. He tried his best to get it on straight. Sometimes he made it, but most nights he went on with the little bow sitting cockeyed, halfway up his neck. Yet, even sitting down drunk, he could out-sing most guys dancing around singing sober.

Ike and Tina's band played behind all of the acts except for Chuck Berry; for some unknown reason, we were asked to back him. Ike told us that Chuck had requested that we back him, although he never spoke a word to any of us. Once in Richmond, Virginia, the downtown audi-torium we were to play that night was near a Sears store. Before the show, I walked over to shop for some new tires for the van and there was Chuck, walking around Sears Roebuck with his overcoat on. He saw me and kind of smiled and grunted a greeting, and for the next thirty minutes we walked around together looking over the many automobile accessories Sears has to offer in absolute silence. That night, in the middle of his set, he turned his back on five thousand people and with a big grin on his face sang "Memphis" to only us—very strange.

After the tour, we played a pick-up date in Charleston, West Vir-ginia, with Pig Meat Markham, the great black vaudeville comic. The show was held in a high school gym with ropes hanging from the ceiling, tethered to the walls by hooks. The stage was set under the basketball goal at one end of the gym. A ladder led up the back wall to an opening in the ceiling high above the stage. During our segment of the show, I laid my horn down in mid-song and climbed up the ladder into the open-ing. I took my clothes off, climbed back down about halfway, unhooked

48

one of the ropes from the wall and swung out over the bewildered audience. I then swung back to the ladder, climbed up, put my clothes on, then climbed back down to the stage, where I picked up my horn and started to play again. This was the beginning of what I later called my vacant years.

We came home for Christmas, and the next day headed for Tulsa to play a week stand at the Fondalite Club, ending with New Year's Eve. The week was uneventful, although I did make a lot of friends, some of whom remain my best friends today. They were all local singers and musicians like Jimmy Markham, Carl Radle, Jimmy Karstein, J. J. Cale, Chuck Blackwell, and Leon Russell. They were a lot like us, playing the same music at local clubs and dances in Tulsa, a town not all that different from Memphis.

I say that week was uneventful, although on New Year's Eve something did happen that had the band starting to worry about me. We had met a few girls that week and two of them showed up at the motel as we were getting dressed for the gig. The weather was freezing and one of the ladies was wearing a floor-length, gold lamé cape that looked like something Elvis or Solomon Burke might wear. We were on the second floor just across from the upstairs restaurant, where well-dressed diners were having their New Year's Eve dinners by candlelight. There was a swimming pool between us and the restaurant, and the water had been left in for the winter. I asked the young lady if I could borrow her cape, threw it over my shoulders, and stood on the top of the railing eye-to-eye with the diners across the pool. The ones nearest the window sat frozen, forks full of hamhocks and black-eyed peas suspended between their plates and mouths as I spread my arms so the light from the pool reflected on the beautiful golden cape. I teetered on the railing for a few seconds and then I was airborne.

I felt like a lone golden eagle for about two seconds, until gravity and the freezing cold water cut short my flight. It was like I had landed in a ravine full of sewing needles and I stood there trapped, chest-high in the numbing waters. Finally, I had to make myself walk, dragging my legs like sacks of concrete to the edge. It took what seemed like an hour to pull myself out of the pool, only to find that the gate to the five-foot-high cyclone fence was locked tight. I stood there shaking like a dog shittin' peach pits until I finally got the strength to drag over a wrought iron table. I climbed on and jumped across the fence, then dragged myself back up to my room, where I lay for thirty minutes in a tub of hot water. No matter how crazy this stunt might seem to me now, I

ROAD STORIES AND RECIPES

remember having a strange feeling of accomplishment that led to other equally astounding feats in the years to come. The vacant years had begun in earnest.

The New Year found Stax in transition. Steve Cropper had been working for Mrs. Axton in the record shop after quitting the band. Chips Moman was still running the studio while Jim Stewart worked his day job at the bank. There had been accusations from local writers who had brought songs in for Chips to listen to that, after turning them down, Chips copyrighted them himself and some of the songs were beginning to show up on various albums recorded at Stax. When Jim confronted Chips with the complaints he had been receiving, Chips stormed out and quit. This made way for Steve to take over the studio and things began to change. There were new faces around the place, like a young tenth-grade keyboard player named Booker T. Jones, and Isaac Hayes, who was working at the Memphis meat-packing plant. There was also a familiar face who started turning up daily at the studio, the great Al Jackson. There was a big change coming on the Memphis music scene, a change that no one involved in the studio ever imagined in their wildest dreams.

With no record on the charts, the New Year looked bleak indeed for the Mar-Keys. We played a couple of short tours in the winter of 1962, but they were starting to be a problem in themselves. There were too many people, too many egos, and less and less money on these tours. When you stopped to think about it, the admission price to these shows was only two or three dollars and it's hard to imagine how anyone made a living playing them. They were also getting to be boring since we played the same three or four songs every night.

There were a couple of highlights that I will never forget. One was on a cold February evening somewhere in the Northeast. I can't remember where, since after a while every town started to look the same to me. We arrived backstage and set up our instruments for that night's show. The PA had been tested by Jerry Butler's trio, which still included Curtis Mayfield on guitar. I wandered around the dark, empty theater and was sitting in the top balcony when everyone left to get a bite to eat. Everyone, that is, but Curtis Mayfield, who stayed on and, alone on the empty stage, gave one of the greatest performances I've ever witnessed. I'm sure he didn't know I was sitting up there in the dark listening to him, 'cause you could tell he was playing and singing to no one but

The Mar-Keys, 1960.

himself. This private performance got so good, I almost cried.

On another night in Erie, Pennsylvania, I remember watching from the wings as Shep and the Limelites incited a riot, clearing the whole place before we even had a chance to play. But for the most part each day was uneventful, playing the same three or four songs every night to what seemed like the same audience. So after the last of these shows we came back South to once again play a string of black nightclubs and road-houses, with an occasional club date in Memphis.

THE BOTTOM

That spring, Ray Brown outdid himself when he booked us for two jobs on the same night. The first gig was to be at a drive-in movie in Truman, Arkansas. We arrived just before dark to find the big neon marquee all lit up. It read, "'Hell is for Heroes,' starring Steve McQueen and Bobby Darrin with the Mar-Keys." The lot was already packed with cars and we drove around looking for a place to set up. After finding none, we went to the concession stand to ask the owners, an elderly couple, what to do. "Where do you want us?" Wayne asked. The old man pointed toward the ceiling. "Up there," he said, in a not-overly-friendly voice. I somehow got the impression he didn't like musicians, rock 'n' roll, or us in general. Since Wayne was from Arkansas, we let him do the talking. The Mom and Pop duo were not impressed. "How do we get up there?" Wayne asked, playing Mr. Nice Guy to the hilt. The old man led us out the back door into the dark and pointed to a ladder propped up against the eaves of the roof. We couldn't believe it. I mean things had been bad before, but climbing a rickety ladder with all our instruments to play on top of a concession stand at a drive-in movie in Truman, Arkansas, was the last straw. It couldn't get any worse, but what the hell, we needed the money and we were far enough from Memphis that maybe none of our family or friends would ever find out. So up we went.

Terry had the hardest job, lugging his drums up to the roof on that shaky ladder. Packey, as usual, was braced for the cool night air with a fifth of Old Charter. At first, he refused to go up and sat in the van sipping from his bottle, but after a lot of coaxing, he too made the climb. Once on top, we faced a sea of automobile roofs and realized our audience was still in their cars, probably waiting for us to start playing. There was only one microphone on the roof, and Wayne quickly took over as front man, putting the old mike to the test. "Testing 1, 2. Testing 1, 2!" he shouted in his best professional tone. Nothing. Once again, Wayne tried. "Mike test 1, 2, 3! Mike test 1, 2, 3!" Still nothing. Now he was riled. "Testing 1, 2! Testing 1, 2!" he screamed. After getting no response on his third try, he grabbed the mike, "You fucking piece of shit!" he growled. These words had barely cleared his lips when about one third of the cars in the place turned on their lights, started their engines and left in a hurry. The old man came running out of the back door of his concession stand, screaming up at us and shaking his fist. "Cut that nasty talkin' out up there. I don't like it one little bit!" Only then did we realize that the mike was working perfectly, and the sound was coming out of the extension speakers into the cars where most of the patrons were families with small children.

After some apologies, we started playing. The roof was slanted at a fifteen degree angle down the back, which made steady footing a problem, especially for Packey, who had trouble standing anyway. He had his bottle sitting by his right foot and walked back to the dark end of the roof to sneak a drink between songs. In the middle of our fourth song, he accidentally kicked the bottle over and it rolled down the roof and over the edge. Packey panicked, cut short his solo, and ran down the roof trying to catch it. In his haste, he misjudged the distance in the dark and followed the bottle over the edge, his saxophone still strapped on. We all stopped playing and rushed to the edge of the roof, expecting to find Packey lying on the ground with a broken neck. Instead we found him sitting propped up against the back of the building, sipping whiskey from the amazingly unbroken bottle. He stared up at us. "I ain't comin' back up there," he said, a look of determination across his face that was barely visible in the dark.

We knew the gig was over. To reinforce this fact, the old man, this time followed by his wife, was on us with a fury. "Ya'll get out of here!" he roared. "I don't allow no drinking on my place. We had the Sunshine Boys band here last month and they didn't get drunk and nasty talk my customers!" He was shaking now. His anger building, he followed us back and forth as we loaded the van, his wife right behind him. As we pulled out, he let go with one more burst. "Ya'll ain't never playing at my drive-in again!" he roared. "Never!" He didn't know how right he was. As we pulled out on the highway, the movie was just starting. If we knew what lay ahead at our second gig that night, we might have stayed and watched the show.

The Cotton Club was a low, cinder-block building on highway 140 outside Lepanto in eastern Arkansas. The parking lot was mostly ruts and mud holes, and it was difficult finding a parking place without fear of drowning. The second I walked in the door of that place, I knew it was trouble. We had played enough roadhouses to know the difference between the dangerous and the lucky-to-get-out-alive ones. This place on the death scale was a good 9.5. I was almost relieved when I saw the reinforced chicken wire surrounding the low stage, although I would have preferred plexiglas. There was no way to cross through the wire from the inside of the club, and the bartender took us back outside and around to a back door that opened onto the bandstand. There was a deadbolt on the inside with which we could lock ourselves in, which we used immediately. There were cushions of all sizes scattered around the large bandstand, which we later figured out were for our comfort when we took breaks. If we needed to go to the restroom all we had to do was unlock our door and step outside. There was a lot to be said about this setup, especially under the circumstances.

Just as we finished setting up, as if on cue, people started pouring in. They were mostly men and looked to be farm workers and day laborers. There were a couple of women who sat down front. One of them had only one leg and, although she couldn't dance that well, she could drink like a whale. She sat there making eyes at Wayne until she passed out on the table. Although there were a few small fights that night, nothing major developed and we were relieved to finish playing and get back to Memphis in one piece.

Things began to fall apart after that. We returned to Miami for a month that April. The record distributor there knew a guy who knew a guy who owned the Atlantique Motel in North Miami Beach and got us a great deal on rooms: two bucks a day per person. It didn't get any better than that, even in the off season. We played a week stand at the Sunrise Club in Fort Lauderdale during spring break. That week was absolutely crazy with too many parties, too much booze, and, for the first time in our short careers, too many women. For the next three weeks we just lay on the beach all day, wondering what to do next. We knew we could not keep up this pace and keep our sanity. Of course, mine had already started to slip, but life on the road really didn't have a lot to do with it.

I had been in the army for about six months and one morning I went down to donate blood in order to get a three-day pass. They gave you a short examination beforehand, and during mine the doctor thought he heard something strange about my heartbeat. He sent me to the hospital for an electrocardiogram and found I had an irregular rhythm to my heart. It was not a continuous thing, it came and went, and I had felt it for years, but had never really worried about it. They put me in the hospital, where I stayed for weeks while they ran test after test trying to determine what was causing this arrhythmia. They never did find out anything and finally sent me packing, a medical discharge in one hand and a sack full of tranquilizers in the other. By the time I got back to Memphis, I was addicted, an addiction that lasted for the next twenty-five years. I didn't realize until years later that the pills were changing the way I acted: irrational acts like jumping into an outdoor swimming pool in the dead of winter or swinging buck naked over a gymnasium full of startled black people. Things got a lot worse before they got better.

In June we returned to Texas (and Mexico) for two weeks. The first three days we played a club in Houston where the house band was led by Johnny and Edgar Winter. The next stop was Galveston, where after the gig we sat around drinking beer and daring each other to go to a famous whorehouse across the bridge in Texas City. Somewhere around 2:30 or 3:00 the beer took control and off we went. We had never been to an American house of ill repute and this one turned out to be a good one to break us in. I had always imagined these places were full of less-than-desirable women with diseases that would rot parts of your body off. I was pleasantly surprised when the ladies of this establishment turned out to be our age and quite pretty.

Wayne and Terry, while in two young ladies' arms, asked them to accompany us to Dallas for the next gig. I don't know if it was the beer or maybe they just got caught up in the moment. Anyway, when we woke up the next morning, our motel parking lot was full of whores, suitcases packed, ready to hit the road. They had their own cars and we caravaned north to Big D for a week's engagement at Luann's Club. Luann's was a sprawling place with three bandstands and a real touch of class. It was one of the nicer nightclubs we had played, and for the first time we didn't have to worry about meeting any girls. We had a great time that week, not knowing it was the last decent gig we would ever play together. Duck had gotten married to his high school sweetheart and she was pregnant. We were barely making enough money to support ourselves, much less a family. We tried one more gig: a month-long stint at a club in St. Paul, Minnesota. It was terrible, and after a couple weeks we packed up and came home. Our van was broken and we rode the train. We were so depressed, we made the eighteen-hour trip almost without speaking. I think everybody must have been thinking about what they were going to do next.

THE LAST HURRAH

Over the next year we played two or three more gigs together when the money was good, but for the most part, the Mar-Keys were history. One of these gigs was New Year's Eve 1963, when we played for a bunch of crazy college students from Lake Forest University, just north of Chicago. Packey had gotten the van repaired and had been using it for transportation, and guaranteed the old bus had one more trip in her. He was half right. We barely made it to Chicago when she gave her last gasp and we had to call the school for help. A group of students came and got us, but refused our request to be taken to a motel. This was actually the day before New Year's Eve, but they were already celebrating and most of them were drunk. They took us to their dorm, insisting we stay the night, which we did. Some of the students I recognized from spring break the year before in Fort Lauderdale, where we had played a week at the Sunrise Club. They really liked the band and came in every night and that's how we were hired for this New Year's Eve bash.

As the night wore on, so did the party and, although they had given us each a room in which to sleep, we didn't get a lot of rest. These people were absolutely insane. They made *Animal House* look like *Cinderella*. After maybe two hours' sleep the next morning, they woke us for lunch, which for most of them was more booze. After all the bars and roadhouses we had played, we had never seen anybody drink like these fools. We returned from lunch to find a line of Greyhound buses parked outside the dorms. "What are they for?" we asked. "To take us to the party, of course," one of them said. Only then did we discover that the party was going to be on Lake Michigan and the buses were there to take us to Milwaukee to board the boat. We left around mid-afternoon, arriving that evening in a caravan of drunken college students who were starting to get a little scary.

The boat was actually a cruise ship with five or six decks and an enormous ballroom. We set up our instruments and were shown to our staterooms to get dressed. The ship pulled out about eight o'clock and we started playing about nine. By this time we had figured it was better to join 'em than to fight 'em, and when midnight came, no one on the boat was feeling any pain except the crew, who stayed well out of the fracas. By the time we had finished playing, the two-day binge started to catch up with the male members of the party and they started falling like flies. The ship sailed across the lake to the Michigan side and started back again. At this point, some of the girls were just getting started and, since their dates were lying unconscious all over the ship, they picked on us to take up the slack.

When the ship docked the next morning, it was all we could do to walk off the boat under our own power, which is more than I can say for most of the students. Some of the walking wounded were carrying a friend fireman style, or some piece of the ship like a life preserver or fire axe. Some of them took it a little further, carrying paintings and plants. I saw one young lady coming down the gangway with a machete and was relieved to see members of the crew take it from her. There were crew members on each side of the gangway and as each person stepped off the boat they were relieved of their bounty. By the time the last person had disembarked, there was a huge pile of goods on either side of the gangway. There was everything from furniture to orthopedic appliances.

In the early morning mist, the whole scene looked more like Dunkirk than Milwaukee and I dreaded the bus ride back to Lake Forest. Most of the people on my bus fell asleep as soon as they sat down, but when we got about twenty-five miles from the school, we had to stop for another bus that had broken down. The people from that bus got on ours and we were packed in like sardines. Before the driver could take his seat behind the wheel, one of the drunker students jumped up and screamed, "I want a piece of this big baby!" He was in the driver seat like a flash, trying to get the bus in gear, while I sat there praying he wouldn't. After some horrific sounds from the transmission, he grabbed a gear and we were off with a lurch. Every time the driver tried to get his bus back, he was screamed down by the students closest to the front. The drunk man did pretty good on the highway, but when we got in to Lake Forest, he got bored. Lake Forest is a well-to-do community with large houses with spacious lawns and I guess the big yards were too much of a temptation. The streets were narrow and he started taking shortcuts across the lawns. I can't imagine what those poor people thought looking out their windows over their morning papers and seeing a Greyhound bus roaring across their front yard.

We finally got back to the school and slept for a few hours that afternoon. All except Packey and Wayne, who sat up drinking with some of the students. They had such terrible hangovers, the only cure was to get drunk again. That night, we were carried to the Greyhound bus station in downtown Chicago by some of these drunken maniacs. Walking into the station was like going to heaven after all we had been through in the past two days. When our bus was called, I was so tired I could barely make it to the gate. Wayne was in line in front of me and was mumbling drunk. When the driver asked him for his ticket, Wayne just stood there, kind of swaying back and forth, his eyes knee deep in water. "What ticket?" he whispered, checking all his pockets and trying to get past the big black man, who didn't like it at all. He finally took Wayne by the arms and put him on the curb. The rest of us had our tickets in hand, but we were so gone, we didn't care about anything. As the bus pulled out of the station we saw Wayne trying to make it back inside the terminal. One step up and two steps back. I figured the best thing that could happen to him was to be arrested. That way, he could sleep it off without being murdered, but he turned up in Memphis the next day, not knowing how he got there.

57

58

The Mar-Keys, 1964. <u>Left</u> <u>to</u> <u>right</u>: Don Nix, Terry Johnson, Duck Dunn, Steve Cropper, Packey Axton, Wayne Jackson.

STAX OF HOT WAX

BEATNIKS, BURKLES, AND THE BITTER LEMON

I rented a one-room apartment on Poplar just across the street from Overton Park. Overton is Memphis's answer to Central Park in New York City. It's a beautiful place with acres and acres of unspoiled woodlands smack in the middle of town. There's an eighteen-hole golf course on one side and a beautiful old zoo on the other. Right in the middle of the park was the Memphis Art Academy, which drew students from all over the country. Most of these students were what some people called Beatniks in 1963, and were the leading edge of the coming hippie movement. But these folks were more committed than the future hippies, living a lifestyle contrary to everything so-called normal people lived. Most of the out-of-town students lived along Poplar Avenue and walked to school across the park. I was playing sax five nights a week at a roadhouse in south Memphis from nine until three in the morning. The bass player in this band was Mike Leech, my old garage-band buddy. Some mornings I went to the park after the gig and just sat until the sun came up.

It was on one of these early morning respites that I met Lydia Saltzman, the queen of the Memphis underground. She lived just up the street in a coldwater flat with only a mattress on the floor. We became friends. I don't think she had ever met anyone like me; I sure as hell had never met anyone like her. Lydia introduced me to other students, most of whom were my age and shared a common interest. None of us had any plans whatsoever about what we were going to do with the rest of our lives and not one of us really cared. These people really changed my life. They introduced me to John McIntire, the sculpture teacher at the art academy. John was like no one I had ever met—a true artist who remains a friend of mine to this day.

He opened a coffeehouse down the street called the Bitter Lemon, which became a gathering place for people who shared the same interests as my new friends and me. It seemed at last I had found a niche and spent most of my time with these people. The Mar-Keys and the road seemed a million miles away. I finally quit the roadhouse gig and spent all my time hanging out at the park or at the Bitter Lemon. We ate our

61

meals at a neighborhood restaurant called Burkle's Bakery. It was a family-owned place and probably the best soul-food restaurant I've ever eaten in. The owners were a middle-aged brother and sister who didn't mind when we came in in the afternoon and sat for a couple of hours ordering nothing but a glass of iced tea and a piece of spice cake. They knew we would be back the next day for lunch and a late supper before heading to the Bitter Lemon for a night of local blues, folk, and rock 'n' roll. The Lemon closed around midnight, and we returned to the park and ran wild in the darkness 'til the sun came up.

I rarely saw my old bandmates until one day Wayne Jackson called. "You want to go to California?" he asked. "When you leaving?" I replied. "I'll be by and pick you up in an hour," and we were off. I had kept in touch with my Tulsa friends and now most of them were living in L.A. Leon Russell had rented a small house in Hollywood and Jimmy Markham was living there with him. Jimmy had been after me for months to come out and see what California had to offer. Wayne and I drove out in his Nash Rambler and I almost felt like Dean Moriarity heading for the promised land. I lived with Jimmy and Leon through the summer of '63 until my money ran out and I had to call home for a bus ticket. That summer was like no other I had ever spent. I knew if I had a future, California would be a big part of it.

I came home broke with no job and took a room in John McIntire's two-story house on Madison, two blocks from my old apartment. I lived on the ground floor next to John's studio, where, every day after his teaching job at the art academy, he worked day and night on a sculpture of Jesus Christ, which Elvis's bodyguards had commissioned for the King's birthday. I sat and watched John chisel away on a piece of stone until the Christ figure emerged and it was beautiful. It still stands over Elvis's gravesite at Graceland.

John didn't have time to run the Bitter Lemon full-time, so he hired a Mississippi poet named Charles Elmo (aka Charlie Brown) to run it for him. Charlie and I became close friends and he turned me on to a lot of the old Delta blues singers, guys like Fred McDowell, Bukka White, Gus Cannon, and Furry Lewis. He hired them on weekends and I sat spellbound while these old masters sang and played the blues. Some nights I went with Charlie to take them home and, after being invited in, we sat all night drinking wine and smoking dope, listening to blues until dawn.

I had seen Furry sweeping streets while I worked as a stockboy at TG&Y, a five-and-dime store downtown. He pushed a barrel on wheels

Don Nix and Furry Lewis in Furry's apartment
on Hernando Street, Memphis, TN, 1965.

and swept the gutters with a push broom. His route was South Main and Beale Street. After work he took his guitar, which he carried on the back of his cart, and played and sang on a bench in Handy Park. He lived two blocks away in a two-room apartment above a grocery store and I started visiting him regularly. I went by at least twice a week to sit all night while Furry played and sang for me and anyone else who dropped by. There was a washboard player across the hall named Goodkid who had played with the Memphis Jug Band in the '30s. He was one of the funniest men I had ever met, and I spent many a night listening to Furry and Good-kid tell road stories and singing blues.

In the spring of 1964, CBS came to Memphis to film a music anthology on early Memphis music. They wanted to film the original Memphis Jug Band and chose the Bitter Lemon for the location. The surviving members of this group were Will Shade, Goodkid, Little Laura

Dukes, and Gus Cannon. Charlie Brown got in touch with Laura and Gus and Goodkid, but when we tried to visit Will Shade in his third-story apartment on Beale, we were stopped by well-meaning neighbors who told us Will was sick and could not have visitors. They wanted to make sure Will died in peace, which he did a week later. Charlie called on Furry to fill out the band, and what a band it was! Furry played guitar, Gus played banjo and blew on a brass jug he wore on a rack around his neck. Laura Dukes played ukulele sporting her trademark brown-and-white saddle oxfords, while Goodkid kept a steady rhythm on the washboard. Goodkid had had a couple of drinks before the gig to settle his nerves since he had never been on national television before. They played two or three songs to warm up and let the TV crew get a sound balance.

After the sound was right, the huge klieg lights were turned on, illuminating the small coffeehouse like a heliport. As soon as the harsh lights came on, the old tired eyes of the band members shut down and they all stopped playing, covering their faces with the back of their hands. This startled the TV crew and the place fell as quiet as a graveyard. After a couple of seconds, Goodkid leaned forward, placing his lips against the microphone nearest him. "Let's turn the lights way down low," he said in a deep, clear, booming voice that almost deafened the guy at the soundboard who was wearing earphones. He was a black man from New York who took offense at his brother of color acting this way. After a huddle with the other members of the crew, Goodkid was asked to leave the stage and was banished to the parking lot. Charlie and I went out to console him. He was sitting on the front fender of my green and white '55 Pontiac. He looked at me and Charlie, tears rolling down his face. "I played all over," he said in a quiet voice. "I even played in Kansas City, but I ain't never been asked to leave no place." It was all Charlie and I could do to keep from going back inside and stomping a mudhole in a few of these guys' asses.

To top it off, when the TV special was broadcast, the Memphis Jug Band was left on the cutting room floor; the old blues singers were screwed again. I think they had come to expect it, and maybe that's why they sang the blues. There were less than twenty people that night in the coffeehouse for the very last performance of one of the legendary groups of early blues. I am truly glad to have been one of them. It was an honor to be in the company of these great artists and it's a night I will never forget.

ON THE ROAD YET AGAIN

Jimmy Markham called in the fall of '63. He had returned to Tulsa and had formed a band that he hoped to take back to California to play the clubs in Hollywood, places like the Red Velvet, P.J.'s, and the Peppermint Lounge. He asked me to meet him in Lawton, an army town in southern Oklahoma not far from the Texas line, where he hoped to woodshed for a couple of months before heading west. Jimmy had put together a tight five-piece group with Bill Boatman on drums, Tommy Tripplehorn on guitar, Gerald Goodwin on bass, Sammy Dodge on tenor, and Jimmy on trumpet; he was doing most of the vocals. When I joined the group a week later, I shared vocals and played tenor.

We played a club downtown, The Cavalier, which was all right on weekdays, but the weekends brought out the soldiers and the crazies. There was a cheap hotel across the street where on Saturday night the GIs lined up through the lobby and down the street to sample the wares of the young ladies upstairs. It was a nasty little town where vice was the main industry. The money wasn't bad, but after a couple of weeks we were ready to move on to California. Also, Jimmy and I had started getting arrested when we showed up downtown during the day. They took us to jail for a couple of hours then let us go without an explanation of why we had been picked up in the first place. We wondered, with all the unlawful acts going on around town, why they would pick on us when we had done nothing wrong. It finally dawned on us that maybe they wanted a payoff to keep working in their town. We never did come up with the money.

One night the sheriff's daughter, who was one of our biggest fans and who kept us supplied with pills, told us the cops were going to bust us the next morning while we slept. I have no idea if she was telling the truth, but we were taking no chances. After the gig that night, we went back to the motel where we had been staying and cleared out.

We headed west and were relieved to cross the Texas border at Texola early the next morning. We picked up Route 66 in Amarillo in our four-car caravan, which included a '52 Ford, a '53 Ford, a '55 Ford station wagon, and my beat-up '58 Thunderbird. We looked more like *The Grapes of Wrath* than a rock-'n'-roll band. I was traveling alone in the T-bird, and when I stopped that afternoon for gas, the others went ahead and I lost them. I enjoyed driving across Texas and New Mexico by myself. There was surprisingly little traffic that time of year on Route 66 and I loved the bigness and the solitude of the desert. We had agreed to drive straight through, but by two o'clock the next morning, with no

65

one to help me drive, I started looking for a motel, which in those days were few and far between. A few minutes later, I came up behind Jimmy, who was parked by the side of the highway out of gas. Tommy Tripplehorn was asleep in the passenger seat, where we left him. There were no service stations in that part of the desert, but Jimmy said he had seen a house a few miles back.

We backtracked a while and sure enough there was a small road off the highway leading into the dark desert. It was a crystal clear night with a million stars but no moon, and the temperature was in the low 30s. We pulled into the road and had traveled about half a mile before we came to a small frame house covered in tar paper that looked a lot like the house on *Sanford & Son.* There was junk scattered everywhere: large wooden spools that had held some sort of cable, three or four cars on blocks, and stacks of stuff covered in plastic anchored with sandstone. There was an old tractor in the yard and five or six washtubs hanging on the side of the house. We also spotted a gas pump, so we pulled up and stopped and were about to get out when at least twenty dogs of all shapes and sizes came running out of the darkness. They were jumping up on the windows, barking and growling, looking like they hadn't eaten for a while. We were about to back out and leave when lights started coming on throughout the house. A dark-skinned man in night clothes stepped out the door and waved for us to come in. I rolled down my window just far enough to yell something out about being dog food. He stepped a little closer, telling us not to worry about his dogs—they wouldn't hurt us.

We got out and walked to the door, a sea of dogs surrounding us, jumping up, licking our face, hands, everywhere. By the time we reached the house, we were soaking wet. The man's wife was behind him now and they were both grinning like possums. We entered the amazingly neat little house, which had a European look to it, and were treated like long-lost relatives. They even woke their three daughters, who offered to fix us something to eat, which we refused, so they passed around a bowl of fresh fruit, which I'm sure was hard to come by in the desert. After spending about twenty minutes sitting around chatting like we had known each other all our lives, the man filled our gas can free of charge, although we did manage to sneak the younger daughter some money before we left. The whole family stood outside waving, the dogs yelping and jumping around until we were out of sight. I knew these people were not of American descent and asked Jimmy where he thought they were from. He said he was sure they were gypsies, but I told him I had always heard that gypsies took things away from you, not the other way around. We got back to Jimmy's car and got it running and resumed our trip west. I got to thinking about it as the sun was coming up and figured it must have been space aliens sent to help us in the dark. I was sure that if I went back to that same place in the daylight, I wouldn't find a soul.

When I arrived the next day, I ran into Billy Lee Riley, an old friend from Memphis who had recorded for Sun Records in the '50s. He had moved to California to advance his recording career, but things had not worked out so well and he was working as a painter. Billy Lee has always been a quiet, generous man and invited me to stay at his house in Hollywood 'til I could find a place of my own. It was an old house, and one morning after he had gone to work, the ancient floor furnace malfunctioned and gas filled the room where I was sleeping. No one knows how long I slept like that and it was a miracle Billy got sick and came home early around noon. He told me later that when he found me I had no pulse and he thought for sure I was dead. He carried me into the front yard, where I finally came around, so sick I could barely walk for two days. As far as I know that's the closest I've come to dying. It's also the reason I live in an all-electric house today.

After a couple of weeks, Jimmy found us a gig in the valley in a small club where we played from nine to four, and after a two-hour break, from six 'til ten in the morning. It was torture and we barely lasted two weeks. The only thing that saved us on these marathon nights was all the people who came down to sit in: Leon, Carl Radle, Chuck Blackwell, Gram Parsons, Delaney Bramlett, and many others. We did play one decent gig at the Peppermint Lounge, but horn bands were on the way out and we finally ended up on 8th Street in downtown L.A. at a club called Peacock Alley. We played there almost two weeks, but it was so bad that one night while I was driving Tommy Tripplehorn home, he and I decided to escape, get the hell out, and never play a sleazy nightclub again. We went home, picked up our belongings, and left, not letting anyone know we were leaving. I think we were afraid they would try to talk us out of it, promising things would get better, but we knew different.

By four o'clock we were in the desert, the windows rolled down, the wind carrying us home. I felt great. I drove and Tommy slept until two o'clock the next afternoon, when outside Kingman, Arizona, my muffler fell off. I pulled out onto the desert, crawled under the car, and with a coat hanger secured the muffler to the underside of the T-bird. In the process, I burned both of my hands on the hot metal and filled the back of my shirt and pants with sand. I was miserable. I woke Tommy, who had been sleeping for hours. "Your turn to drive," I said, and crawled into the small back seat for some well-deserved rest. Tommy looked over the passenger seat, his eyes a beautiful shade of red. "I don't drive," he said, sort of apologetic. "What do you mean you don't drive?" I demanded. "I don't know how," he said. "I don't even have a driver's license." "Why didn't you tell me that before we left?" I replied, my voice taking on a sense of urgency. "You didn't ask me," Tommy said, and I could have killed him. I got back in the driver's seat and, twenty-eight hours later, I dropped him off at his house in Tulsa. He did invite me in for some sleep, but I was too wired and drove the four hundred miles to Memphis in record time. I had just made the approach to the Memphis-Arkansas bridge when the T-bird gave up, never to run again. By this time I had decided that I didn't want to be rich and famous anymore.

John McIntire kept my room vacant at his house so I'd always have a place to stay when I came home. He gave me an old guitar and I learned enough songs to do some solo gigs at the Bitter Lemon.

My tranquilizer addiction continued and, in 1963, my doctor put me on a new pill called Valium that was supposed to be nonaddictive. We found out together just how wrong that piece of information was. My gigs at the Bitter Lemon sometimes included long, rambling impromptu monologues with a few songs thrown in. I soon became better known for my comedy than my singing, and no one knew it was Valium-induced mood swings that were doing all the talking. I did pick-up gigs once in a while with local bands in and around Memphis playing sax. I made enough money to barely get by, but at that point in my life that's really all I wanted to do: get by. I have never placed too much importance on money and it's never been something I had to have to be happy. I rented a small apartment for $50 a month near Overton Park, next door to my friend Lydia Saltzman and, although I lived in other states, even other countries, over the next ten years, I kept this one-room flat as a place of my own that I could always call home.

One of the friends I had met at the Bitter Lemon was Jim Dickinson, who introduced me to John Fry. John was the only child of a wealthy east Memphis family and had built a small studio in the garage of his parents' home. I went there on occasion to try and figure out the recording process, something I had never taken any particular interest in. I was intimidated by all of those knobs and meters and thought they looked too complicated. Besides, I felt more comfortable in the studio than in

Steve Cropper and Don Nix in New York, 1964.
The Nehrus were out of style before we got back
to the hotel.
Photo: Duck Dunn.

the control room. In 1966 John built a state-of-the-art studio on
National Avenue and called it Ardent Recording. John gave me a key to
his new studio and taught me how to use it. I was free to come and go as
I pleased, experimenting in the studio when it was not in use. I was
spending half my time in California, where Leon also let me work in his
Skyhill studio. Between the two, I was learning not only how to engineer
from John, but how to produce from Leon. I didn't know at the time
just how valuable these experiences were. At the time, I was just having
fun and not thinking about making money at it.

BURN, BABY, BURN

The very last gig the original Mar-Keys played together was in August
1965. We got back together at Mrs. Axton's request to play a concert in
Los Angeles with some of the other Stax artists to record a live album at
the Five-Four Ballroom. Our main purpose was to be the backing band
for some of the acts: Rufus and Carla Thomas, William Bell, the Mad-
Lads, and the Astors. Steve Cropper wanted to play guitar so Charlie

Freeman remained in Memphis. We had gone down to the Mississippi River on a Sunday afternoon to have some photos taken a few months before. It was the last time we were photographed together.

The show was being promoted by WGFJ, an L.A. radio station whose top jock was The Magnificent Montague, a real jive ass who (like a lot of disc jockeys at that time) thought he was responsible for the music, giving no credit to writers, artists, or any other creative people associated with making records. Come to think of it, it's a misconception still alive in most places.

Montague was also going to be the emcee for the show at the Five-Four. We stayed at the Hyatt House on Sunset Boulevard. The Hyatt had gotten a reputation as the place to stay in L.A., and you could see almost anyone and everyone in the restaurant at all hours. We only had one rehearsal, but since we knew most of the songs we just ran through the show a couple of times for the recording engineers to get a sound balance. The Five-Four Ballroom was at the corner of 54th and Broadway in the heart of Watts. Like many other times, we were the only white people in the place besides Chuck Blackwell and Carl Radle, who had come down to watch the show. The place was packed with people on the stairs and spilling into the street.

Montague started the evening off by stepping to the mike and pulling a book of matches from his pocket. He lit one, held it over his head, and screamed, "BURN, BABY, BURN!" The place went absolutely crazy and all at once everyone in the place was holding a lighter or match above their heads, chanting in unison, "BURN, BABY, BURN!" Duck and I looked at each other. This was going to be a long night. As Montague introduced each act he lit a match, "BURN, BABY, BURN!" At the end of each song, he yelled "BURN, BABY, BURN!" and before long things started getting scary. I looked down by the side of the stage, where Carl and Chuck were sitting, and saw them heading for the exit. As soon as our part of the show was over, we followed them, getting the hell out of Watts.

For the next week I stayed at Leon's and watched on TV as the people of Watts did exactly what The Magnificent One had told them to do. After the riots, the tapes of the concert were brought back to Memphis to mix but were never released. We learned later that the Watts riots started at the corner of 54th and Broadway.

Gary Lewis, Don Nix, and Sam the Sham, 1967.
Photo: Carl Radle.

IF DICK ONLY KNEW

One of 1965's biggest hit records was "This Diamond Ring" by Gary Lewis and the Playboys. A local L.A. band of mostly inexperienced musicians, they were discovered playing at Disneyland by a former janitor at Liberty Records, Snuff Garrett. Although Snuff's name appeared on the record as producer, the sessions were all Leon Russell. Since the Playboys were young with no road experience, Leon augmented the group with some of the more seasoned musicians from Tulsa. Most of them were living at Leon's house and I guess he figured putting them on the road with Gary Lewis was a good way of getting rid of them. Jimmy Karstein played drums, Carl Radle bass, and Tommy Tripplehorn, who had returned to California, was on guitar. The only surviving members of the old band were John West, who played something called a cordavox, and Gary himself. They turned out to be a really good band who could duplicate the records on stage almost perfectly. "This Diamond Ring" was followed by a string of hits, all conceived by Leon, who was getting a name around Hollywood as the best arranger, producer, and keyboard player in town.

On my many trips to L.A. I always stayed at Leon's house and attended some of the Playboy's sessions. Gary and I became good friends, and since I already knew Carl, Jimmy, and Tommy, he asked me to

Brian Hyland, 1968.
Photo: Don Nix.

accompany them on a Dick Clark Caravan of Stars Tour in the fall of 1966. Some of the other acts on that tour were Jimmy Clanton, Bobby Hebb, Brian Hyland, the Yardbirds with Jeff Beck and Jimmy Page on guitars, and my old friend from Memphis, Sam the Sham and his band the Pharaohs. The tour got off to a roaring start when Jeff Beck snapped the first week in Brownsville, Texas. In the middle of the Yardbirds' set, he started stalking around stage beating on his guitar strings with his volume full up. The audience thought it was part of the show until he stood at the edge of the stage, spitting on the first few rows. He then ran down to his dressing room, locked the door, and refused to come out. When the security people finally got the door open, he went into a rage and started breaking everything in sight, using the Telecaster Jimmy Page had given him. The guitar was his prized possession and he refused to let anyone touch it. By the time he was subdued it was completely destroyed. He was taken to the hospital, where he stayed until he was well enough to return to England.

One of my favorite people on this tour was Brian Hyland. Brian was one of those people whose life is always a mess, but it did not bother him in the least. His first hit a few years earlier, "Itsy Bitsy Teeny Weeny Yellow Polka-Dot Bikini," was a complete fluke. Brian lived with his parents in Lynbrook, New York, and his next-door neighbor had built a small studio in his basement. The neighbor wrote the song and recorded the music track, but had no one to sing it. One day he spotted 15-year-old Brian next door playing in his backyard. He called him over and asked if he would like to try his hand at singing. After the record became a smash, Brian attended a special school in New York City for kids in the entertainment business. After his first tour, he returned home to find his parents had moved to Florida without telling him, and he has been on his own since. If the airlines lost someone's luggage, it was Brian's. If the hot water didn't work in someone's hotel room, it was his. He just had that kind of luck. The great thing about him was that he didn't care. No matter what happened, he was always the same: good natured, easygoing, and one of the funniest guys I've ever known, and I've known some funny ones. When things didn't go quite right for him, he always made a joke about it and kept right on going.

Once in Davenport, Iowa, we spent the night in a hotel that didn't have a restaurant, so we walked a couple of blocks down the street to another hotel that had a coffee shop in one corner of the lobby. It was a nice little place with big plate-glass windows and very few customers. There were four or five of us in the group, which included Gary Lewis, Jimmy Karstein, Tommy Tripplehorn, Brian, and me. We had all ordered our breakfast and everyone but Brian had been served. While we were eating, the manager came over and in a calm voice asked us to leave. He told us there was a small fire in the kitchen and, for our safety, we should exit the building as soon as possible. Since there was no sign of smoke, we decided to stick around and finish our food. Brian jokingly said he thought it was probably his breakfast burning that caused the fire.

As it turned out, he was exactly right. We had almost finished eating when a man in a cook's outfit came running through the kitchen door with a large cloud of smoke following him. Before we could get up and leave, a fire truck came roaring up outside. We ran across the street and watched as the old hotel started to burn in earnest. That night, as we were leaving after the gig, the bus passed by the still-smoldering building. Brian was sure he had caused the whole thing, just by ordering breakfast.

Although the tour was billed as the Dick Clark Caravan of Stars, ol' Dick only showed up in the larger cities, where he emceed the show. In Chicago, a few nights after the Davenport fire, Dick introduced Brian before he was ready to come on stage. The backstage area of the theater was old, dark, and dusty and, as Brian was trying to get to the stage by the shortest possible route, he ran into a brick wall, which he mistook

Jimmy Page, Sam the Sham, Don Nix,
Tommy Tripplehorn, 1967.
Photo: Carl Radle.

in the dark for a free-hanging curtain. He was knocked cold. He landed just out of sight of the audience on the opposite side of the stage from where Gary Lewis was standing. While the band was playing Brian's introduction and everybody was waiting for him to appear, Gary spotted him lying on the floor across the stage. Thinking that he was just fooling around, Gary ran over and grabbed Brian under the arms, dragging him out on the stage in front of ten thousand people, completely unconscious. In the harsh stage lights, you could see the thick layer of dust on Brian's face and coat. You could also see that he was in no condition to perform that night. So the curtain came down on another chapter of Brian Hyland's luck.

On any tour he was on, Jimmy Karstein was always the postgig entertainment director, the host with the most, the master of ceremonies of some of the most bizarre and fun-filled evenings I've ever spent. This tour was no different and, every night after the gig, we congregated in Jimmy's room to drink beer, smoke dope, and listen to one of the best blues record collections still in existence. Karstein hated motel rooms and carried his own props and entertainment in a special suitcase that was always with him. It included a small record player, over one hundred 45s, colored lightbulbs, and his own favorite wall accessories.

Most of the English guys stayed to themselves, until one night Jimmy Page wandered into Jimmy's room in Indianapolis and never left. He was back every night smoking dope, listening to blues, and generally soaking up some good ol' Southern rock-'n'-roll hospitality. Karstein turned him on to amyl nitrate, and Page didn't know whether to kiss him or kill him, but he always came back for more.

THE WICKED PICKETT

After the tour I returned to my one-room flat in Memphis for Christmas. I still hung out almost every night at the Bitter Lemon or Duck Dunn's house, but spent most days at Stax, where my brother Larry had gone to work as an engineer running their newly acquired mastering lathe. There were a lot of new faces around, like Eddie Floyd, Wilson Pickett, and Sam and Dave. I became good friends with Eddie, and we spent most days wandering from office to office making pests of ourselves with all the secretaries.

The great thing about Stax in those days was a casual family atmosphere that prevailed until its closing in 1975. Artists, writers, and musicians gathered in what seemed daily family reunions while 1960s racially divided Memphis went about its day-to-day business. Everyone at Stax, both black and white, got along seemingly well while recording some of the best music in history. When the occasional asshole did come along, they usually didn't last very long.

The best example of this was Wilson Pickett. They didn't call him the Wicked Pickett for baking cookies. Although he was signed to Atlantic, he came to Stax to record through a special arrangement between Jim Stewart and Jerry Wexler. Pickett was difficult enough when he first came to Stax, but after the success of "Midnight Hour" and several other hits he recorded with the Stax rhythm section, he became impossible. Atlantic would call and book five or six days for him to come down and record. It got to the point where Duck Dunn got violently ill the night before a session with him. I mean, if you couldn't get along with Duck, Cropper, Al Jackson, and Booker T., you couldn't get along with anybody.

After one especially bad session with Pickett yelling, screaming, cussing, and generally being impossible, the group went to Jim Stewart and said "Enough." Jim called Atlantic and told them they'd have to record their acts elsewhere, and I think a lot of people were relieved, since Wilson did not reserve his asshole tendencies for the musicians alone. The

Stax rhythm section worked harder than any musicians I've ever met. They were always the first in the studio and the last to leave. They would do anything humanly possible for any artist they ever worked with.

CHRISTMAS WITH FURRY

I had not been up to see Furry Lewis in a couple of months so I drove downtown one cold night around Christmas to see how he was doing. He still lived above the grocery store on Third Street in a two-room flat. There were two or three other apartments other than Furry's upstairs, with Goodkid, the washboard player, occupying one of them. The rooms were well-heated and I found Furry and Goodkid sittin' around talking and drinking whiskey as I entered the cozy, dimly lit apartment. As always, Furry was boiling chicken necks on a small gas stove in the other room. It seemed you had to boil the bony necks two or three days before they were tender enough to eat, and Furry always had a pot of them

76

Don Nix and Furry Lewis,
Memphis, 1970.
Photo: Jim Chappell.

on the stove. He would share anything he had with you—whiskey, cigarettes, even loan you his guitar—but not once in all the years I knew him
did he ever offer me one of his cooked-to-perfection chicken necks. I
was somehow grateful for this, and made a point of never bringing it up.

I joined the two old blues men for a nightcap and sat around 'til the
wee hours listening to them tell me stories about Beale Street and the
Mississippi Delta. I finally fell asleep on a small bed Furry kept in his
kitchen for just such an occasion. I slept like a baby and dreamed I
swapped my National guitar for six pounds of neckbones. The next
morning, Furry was in a somber mood. I had noticed he hadn't brought
his big Epiphone guitar out from under the bed as he usually did on
most nights, especially when there was company in the house. He was
kind of hung over and sat on the side of his bed rubbing his head and
smoking a Pall Mall. I had known Furry for about four years and had
never seen him this low.

He finally looked up at me. "It's in the pawn shop," he said "been
there for over a month and if I don't get it out they're going to sell it.
If I could get it out I could play me a few little jobs around the holidays.
I need to play some jobs to pay my electric bill." He reached over and
got a cigar box he always kept by his bedside, opened it and handed me
his gas and electric bill. It was three months in arrears, and they were
going to cut his power off on Christmas Eve, which was only two days
away. Also after looking around the kitchen, I noticed that besides the
pot of neckbones on the stove, there was absolutely nothing to eat. I had
heard of the blues, but this was ridiculous.

I left the apartment and drove to the pawn shop on Poplar Avenue
where Furry did business. I only had enough cash to get his guitar out
of hock and nowhere near enough to pay his electric bill, so I drove over
to Stax and started collecting money from anyone I could. Everybody
knew who Furry was and they were glad to help. Isaac Hayes, David
Porter, Eddie Floyd, and the MGs all contributed money to pay for his
bills. I then drove over to see Rufus Thomas, a disc jockey for WDIA,
the black radio station that gave out baskets of food to poor families every
Christmas. I asked Rufus if I could get a basket for Furry. Being an el-
der bluesman himself, he took me down to a large room filled with
bushel baskets of canned goods, hams, rolls, sugar, and coffee. After
loading one of the baskets in my car, Rufus said, "On second thought,
you'd better take two."

So off I went back downtown to Furry's. I drove down Beale Street,
past all the boarded-up buildings that used to house the clubs, bars,

poolrooms, hotels, and brothels that were once the heartbeat of the blues. The street where it all started stood cold and deserted. As I turned left on Hernando at Beale, I passed what used to be the most famous club on that jumpin' street, the Club Handy. I remember standing on the street below the windows and listening to the house band a decade earlier. Sunbeam Mitchell had been the owner, and although we were not allowed in, on hot summer nights he left the windows open in the second-floor club so a small pack of white teenagers could stand and soak up the music of that great band. We stood there 'til about midnight, when the cops finally ran us off.

One night a sax player came walking down the stairs playing the most beautiful music any of us had ever heard. We thought maybe he was coming down to play for us since the band upstairs was in midsong. But he just stood on the corner, his horn pointed skyward, his eyes closed, playing his heart out. After a few minutes Charlie Freeman asked him who he was playing to. He took the horn from his mouth and looked at us, the sax still pointed to the heavens. "The eons and the molecules," he said in a soft, hip tone. He was very high. He returned his attention to his horn and played like an angel 'til someone came down and led him back upstairs. None of us knew what it all meant, but we knew it was heavy. Now all that was gone. Boarded-up blues clubs and boarded-up bluesmen were all that remained. I was all at once very depressed and promised myself to return to California as soon as Christmas was over.

I got to Furry's and hauled his guitar and the baskets of food up to the apartment. Goodkid was there and very drunk, although it was not yet five o'clock in the afternoon. When he saw the guitar and food he started to cry and ran across the hall to his flat, returning a couple of minutes later with two jelly glasses, which he gave to Furry. He had got caught up in the moment and the spirit of giving and Furry thanked him, but handed him back one of the glasses, since it was still half full of Concord grape jelly. I told Furry I'd stop by the next day and pay his electric bill with the money I had collected. Before I left, Furry made me promise to come back the next evening, which was Christmas Eve. I told him I would be there and went to spend the holidays at my folks' house. The next night, I slipped off for a few minutes and returned to Furry's, where I found him sitting in the middle of his bed, the big Epiphone across his lap. There had been some more money left from the electricity bill fund, which I had given Furry. Consequently, there was a half-empty fifth of Ten High on his bedside table and Furry was in a good mood.

Hand-written sign above Furry Lewis's bed.
Memphis, 1964.
Photo: Don Nix.

He asked me to sit down on the side of the bed and after talking for a few minutes Furry became uncharacteristically serious. "I want to thank you for what you've done for me and I want to give you something. I've worked up a song for you and once I play it I won't ever play it for nobody again." He reached over and retrieved his bottleneck from the old cigar box on the bedside table. He then began to play the most soulful rendition of "Silent Night" you could ever hope to imagine. I sat there almost in tears listening to this old bluesman play a song especially for me. It's probably the best Christmas present I'd received to this point in my life and the reason the Christmas of 1967 will always stay with me. Over the years, Furry was in constant need and many other people helped him. Guys like Sid Selvidge, John McIntire, and Charlie Brown played the guitar-out-of-hock game with Furry. But no matter how much you did for Furry, he always did much more for you. As Charlie Brown once said, "Knowing Furry Lewis was like living next door to Leonardo daVinci."

SHOOTOUT AT THE PLANTATION

On the second day of 1968, I flew to L.A. and camped out at the plantation, hosted by his Nibs, Mr. Jimmy Karstein. At that time there was a large contingent of musicians, girlfriends, and squatters living in the two-story frame house in Sherman Oaks. Bobby Whitlock had come out from Memphis and was playing with Delaney and Bonnie, who were also regulars at the house. Taj Mahal and his band were there, as well as Chuck Blackwell, Gram Parsons, and Jessie Ed Davis. J. J. Cale and Bill Boatman took turns staying in the small guesthouse out back. Crazy Colonel Gary Sanders lived in one of the upstairs bedrooms with his girlfriend, who was a titty dancer from Oklahoma City.

There was a party every night and for the most part it was a lot of fun, but things could get dangerous. Like the night Jimmy Markham came in drunk and found his girlfriend in bed with Chuck. He started ranting and raving and threatening to kill the both of them until he woke the Colonel. Sanders came to the top of the stairs a couple of times and yelled down for Markham to be quiet, but Markham was mad and drunk and kept yelling and threatening everyone who was sitting around the living room. Finally, the Colonel had heard enough and he appeared on the stairs wearing nothing but a .38 special, which shocked everyone, most of all Jimmy Markham. It was too late to run so he started looking for something to hide behind. He made a terrible choice, one of Kar-stein's congo drums. The Colonel was through talking and he let go with all six shots. When the shooting was over, Markham dropped the drum and ran out the back door, a walking miracle that he wasn't killed or even hit. Later inspection of the congo drum revealed four bullet holes clean through it. Jimmy Markham was a lucky man indeed.

The war in Vietnam was at its peak and the hippie movement was in full swing, but none of that mattered to anyone at the plantation, espe-cially me. I was still in my self-centered posture, running low to avoid any contact with responsibility. One Sunday afternoon we all went to Griffith Park to a love-in. There were thousands of people there trying to out-hip each other. Almost every one of them was dressed in the uni-form of the day, mostly purchased at the trendy head shops along Sun-set Strip. You could spend a fortune in one of those places trying to look destitute. Of course, we all dressed the part too and were more than happy to take part in the free love portion of the hippie movement, but there was something almost too good about the whole deal.

As I sat there on the hill with Jessie Ed looking down at the thou-sands of dancing merrymakers, I asked him what he thought it was all about. He sat there smoking a joint behind his mirrored aviator sun-glasses. "Freedom, man, freedom," he said with only a trace of sarcasm. I thought about that for a minute and then asked him if he was sure he wanted all of those people to be free to do anything they pleased. He rolled over in the grass laughing like a madman. It was my last love-in.

I visited Leon's studio almost daily, where he was involved in numerous projects, some of which I worked with him on. We wrote and produced several records for Phil Scaff's newly formed and short-lived Independence record label. We cowrote one of Gary Lewis's last records for Liberty, "The Loser." I learned a lot from Leon in those days, watching him do his take-charge, hands-in-the-air routine in almost every studio in Hollywood. He told me once that no matter how many musicians, engineers, or bystanders were in the studio, always walk in like you knew exactly what you were doing and no one would ever doubt you, and he was right. He was a great teacher for anyone who wanted to be a writer/producer and I will always be grateful for the schooling I received from him.

In the summer of 1968, I returned to Memphis and Ardent Studios to see if I could pull it off: make records for artists and musicians and make them think I knew what I was doing. Stax was going stronger than ever and new studios were popping up all over town. The most significant of these was American, which was owned by Chips Moman, our old friend from Stax. Also, Willie Mitchell had opened a studio down the street from Stax that was cutting local R&B acts as well as recording his own band. This was an exciting time in Memphis, probably the most exciting since the Civil War. I still had the one-room flat across from Overton Park, but the friends I had met and hung out with from the art academy had graduated and moved on. The Bitter Lemon was now filled with teenage hippies and the music was more rock 'n' roll than folk and blues.

The best entertainment in town by far was at Duck Dunn's house, where I went nightly after eating at Burkle's. Duck, his wife, June, and two sons, Mike and Jeff, were like my own family. After working all day at the studio, Duck came home, ate, then took his place in the den with the first of many scotch and waters and watched TV, waiting for Johnny. Duck Dunn loved Johnny Carson. Everything on from seven to ten-thirty was just a warmup to the *Tonight Show*, which in those days ran for an hour and a half. June had her place on the couch, while the boys and I sprawled on the floor in front of the TV. Jeff was six and Mike was four, and they were good boys. Duck and his family were close and it was a warm and comfortable home where I spent some of my most happy times.

There was one ritual that played almost the same every evening. Right in the middle of Johnny, the boys and I started a low chant, "We want corn. We want corn. We want corn." It grew in intensity as June joined in, "WE WANT CORN!" Duck, who by this time was on his fourth or fifth scotch, growled something like, "Not now. No way. I'm watching Johnny." But as the chant grew he always succumbed and went to the kitchen to pop a big bowl of popcorn, which we devoured by the handful while Duck watched the rest of Johnny in peace. Great memories.

DON'T LET ME DIE IN TEXAS

It was hard getting started as an independent record producer, even though John Fry was letting me use Ardent at no charge, at least until I sold something. I barely had enough money to live on, much less make records. I had started writing on my own with the old guitar my friend John McIntire had given me, but most of my songs were not R&B enough for Stax and not pop enough for Chips, who by this time was recording acts like Dionne Warwick, B.J. Thomas, and Dusty Springfield at American.

I was getting frustrated and thinking about going back to California when I got a call from Dale Hawkins. He was in town looking for songs for Bruce Channel, whom he was producing for Bell Records. I remembered Dale from his '50s hit "Suzy Q," so I took my guitar and drove downtown to meet him at the old River Bluff hotel. He was a hyper person who had a hard time keeping still, which I learned later was due to an abnormal influx of amphetamines. I didn't like speed myself and never messed with it, but I took an immediate liking to Dale, who had a wide, goofy grin that made him hard to dislike. Even without the pills he was always on the move and his worst enemy was a dull moment. After I had played only one of my songs, Dale jumped up. "That's what we need," he yelled. "Let's go to Nashville and cut it." I asked him when he would like to leave and he looked at me like I was crazy. "Right now, man. Let's get it while the gettin's good!" and we were off.

He had a brand new Cadillac Coupe deVille and drove like a man possessed. I had never seen anything like it. He told stories, waving his arms around like a Baptist preacher. He pulled papers out of his briefcase, reading them to me, all the while driving ninety miles an hour up I-40. I was relieved when we pulled into Nashville and swore to myself I would take the bus home. We checked into a motel, and he spent most of the night calling studios and musicians. He read stuff, wrote stuff down, paced up and down, anything to keep from going to sleep. I always believed he was afraid to go to sleep. I had heard of people with such fears. People who thought if they went to sleep they might not wake

Dale Hawkins, New York City hotel room, 1968.
Photo: Don Nix.

up; maybe Dale just figured if he went to sleep he might miss something.

The next morning we were in the studio cutting tracks for Bruce Channel's album. He had recruited some of Nashville's top musicians, including J. D. Fontana on drums, who was a pleasure to work with. About four o'clock that morning, Dale had bumped me upstairs from songwriter to coproducer, so at ten the same morning I found myself producing tracks on an artist who was not present. When I asked Dale questions like what key the song should be in, he told me, "It don't matter man. This cat's got a range you won't believe." We cut three or four tracks that day, none of which were ever used.

After the session, Dale insisted I ride back to Memphis with him and we finally struck a deal. I drove. I woke up the next afternoon in my own bed wondering what the hell had just happened. I didn't have long to wonder, for two days later Dale called. "There's a first-class ticket at the American Airlines counter. We're going to finish the album in Tyler, Texas." I asked where Tyler was, a little relieved I was flying and not riding with him. "It's ninety miles south of Dallas, man, and it's a great little studio. You're gonna love it." So I flew down to Dallas the next afternoon, not knowing what to expect. Dale picked me up at Love Field, one of my all-time favorite airports. We drove out to the suburbs to a large ranch-style house, with beautiful trees and a manicured lawn. In the brief time I had known Dale, he had never mentioned his private life and I was surprised to find he was married to a sweet, beautiful woman and had two great-looking kids. He was a completely different person around his family and I immediately had a new respect for him.

The next morning we were off again, driving down to Tyler, speeding in more ways than one. Bruce came down the next day. I had met him in Tulsa, where we had played some gigs together at the Peppermint Lounge on the notorious corner of 11th and Denver, along with Jimmy Markham and Jimmy Karstein. I loved his megahit "Hey Baby." It had been one of my favorite records and I was excited to work with him. Dale was right: The little studio in Tyler was fantastic. It was owned and operated by the local president of the John Birch Society, Robinhood Brian. The musicians were shipped in from Dallas and were the only weak point in the overall scene, but what they lacked in ability they made up in persistence and we got four tracks in two days.

I thought we were on a roll, but Dale was bored with Tyler and suggested a trip to New York, where he said he could get me a job as staff producer with Bell Records. We drove back to Dallas late that night. It was a clear night and we were the only car on the highway. Right outside of Dallas in a wide spot in the road called Forny, Texas, the Caddy quit. We were rolling along having a big time when all at once the motor stopped and the lights went off, a complete electrical breakdown. Being the quick thinker he was, ol' Dale shifted it into neutral and we coasted into a truck stop.

I thought it was a great stroke of luck to make it to a place that was open all night, but the feeling of security vanished the second I walked through the door. The place was filled with truck drivers and farmers having an early breakfast. Now Dale always dressed like a businessman with slacks and jacket and short-cropped hair, but no one was looking at Dale. All eyes were on the long-haired hippie communist bastard behind him. The whole place fell silent except for the noise from the kitchen, and I realized, three steps too late, that long hair was a major crime in Forny, Texas, one I was sure carried the death penalty.

I had to think fast. Running was out of the question. Even if I could get away, where could I hide out there in the Texas flatlands with the sun coming up? There was a sign that read "Wait to be seated by hostess," but no hostess was forthcoming, and Dale and I just stood there like a couple of dummies in a shooting gallery rattling the change in our pockets. I happened to notice a glass counter to my left packed with bright shiny new firearms of all sizes and calibers. I went into my there's-some-thing-real-bad-wrong-with-me-and-I'm-not-responsible-for-my-actions routine. I walked the few steps over to the counter, dragging my right foot, my body racked with mini-convulsions and my head shaking with a palsy-like motion. I stole this from an old woman who lived down the street from us when I was a kid who suffered from a disease called Saint Vitus's dance.

When I got to the counter, I turned to Dale, who was still waiting to be seated. "CAN I HAVE A GUN, DADDY?" I said in a loud voice.

Dale shot right back, "No son, you don't need another gun."

We were seated immediately and the place went back to business as usual and no one gave us even the slightest glance while we sat and had breakfast. As we walked across the parking lot to the Caddy, which need-ed only a fuse, Dale said to me, "Man, we oughta take this act on the road!" I told him, "We are on the road brother, and sometimes it scares the shit out of me."

Back in Dallas that afternoon, we flew to New York for a big deal meeting with Larry Uttal, Bell Records' president. We stayed at the Americana Hotel and for three days ordered room service, courtesy of Bell Records. Not once did I lay eyes on Larry Uttal. I had been to New York City a few times before with Steve Cropper and Duck and had met a few friends I visited with, but other than that the whole trip was a waste of time.

I flew back to Memphis alone, joining Dale and Bruce two weeks later to finish up the album in Tyler. We checked back into the Holiday Inn while Bruce made the ninety-mile drive to and from Dallas each day. On the second night of recording, Dale drove me to the motel about 2 A.M. After an especially hard day in the studio, I went to my room and went straight to bed and slept for nine hours. I got up and phoned the front desk for Dale's room to see if he wanted to eat before going to the studio.

The lady asked me to hold for a minute when a man who identified himself as the assistant manager asked me, "Are you with Mr. Hawkins?" I replied in the affirmative and asked him if there was anything wrong. The man paused for a few seconds. "Mr. Hawkins phoned the desk at four o'clock this morning and asked the night manager to drive him to the hospital, and I assume he's still there."

I got dressed and went outside and saw the Caddy parked where we had left it the night before. I had a key, so I got directions and drove quickly to the hospital, wondering why Dale had not called me if he had taken ill. The hospital was more of a clinic in a couple of double-wide trailers and didn't look like a place you would like to be taken to with anything worse than a cold. I inquired at the desk if they had a Mr. Dale Hawkins in their care. They asked if I were a relative, to which I quickly lied, "Yes, I'm his brother, may I see him?" After some whispering among the nurses present, I was led down a hall marked "Emergency," then into a small room where Dale lay on a gurney wrapped in a thermal blanket, an ugly-looking device that pumps cold water through coils that are laced through a grey canvas blanket, reminding me of a large cocoon.

Dale looked awful. His head was swelled up like a beachball. He was unconscious and I thought for a moment he was dead. A voice from behind me said, "Dale is very sick," and I turned to see his wife sitting in the corner, her eyes red from crying. "What's wrong with him?" I asked, stunned by this whole bizarre scene. "They don't know, but his blood pressure has been as high as 300 over 200 and they told me there's a chance he might not live." Hell, with a blood pressure like that, it was a miracle he wasn't already dead.

I had to get out of there. This was way too much to deal with before breakfast. After mumbling something about calling me if there was anything I could do, I quick-stepped outside, where Bruce was standing on the small lawn. I walked over and asked how he had heard about Dale. "I've just been to the studio and Robinhood told me he was here. Do they know what's wrong with him?" Bruce asked, sounding concerned.

"Well, nobody's saying anything, but it has all the earmarks of an overdose to me," I said.

The look of concern left his face. Bruce is a meat-and-potatoes man, rock solid, and what you see is what you get, but he is no prude. He didn't mind people drinking or even taking drugs, but when it interfered with the business at hand, he had no time for it. He stood there for a few seconds then looked up at me. "We gonna cut?" he said like a man who had driven a hundred miles to work and didn't want it to all be in vain. "Why not?" I said, and we were off to the studio.

We worked most of the afternoon, but our hearts weren't in it. We called the clinic every couple of hours to check on Dale, but there wasn't much change. I caught a ride back to Dallas with Jay Pruitt, one of the musicians working on the sessions whom I had gotten to be friends with, and someone I worked with many times over the next few years. I flew back to Memphis and called Bruce to see if he had heard anything about Dale. He told me they had brought him back to Dallas in an ambulance and he was in serious but stable condition. Bruce told me he was going to England the next day to stay for the rest of 1968, which he did.

Later, after Dale recuperated, he flew over and they finished the album in London. It was released at Christmas with only a smattering of applause and I never heard from Dale again. I did hear from a friend a few years later that he had gotten his life straight and was working as a drug counselor in a rehab hospital in Little Rock. Bruce married an English girl and lives down the street from me. I saw him in Kroger's the other night, getting milk.

So I was back in Memphis hanging around Ardent and Stax in the day and watching Johnny with Duck and his family at night, wondering where I could get enough money together to make some records. I finally realized all I needed was a self-contained band that wanted to make a record and didn't expect to be paid for it. I would supply the studio and they the music. I experimented with local acts, being producer and engineer on most of these sessions. I managed to fumble through three albums ranging from folk to pop to uninspired blues. The results were less than memorable, although Stax bought them all. By the time I paid Fry for the studio time, I had $60 left. At this rate, I would have to get a bigger truck. The only good thing to come out of these sessions, besides a little fun, was that Jim Stewart offered me a job as staff writer and producer at Stax, with a combined salary of almost $50,000 a year.

In December I was sitting in my flat listening to records on a cold, dreary evening when Sam the Sham called me. "Have you heard about Otis and the MGs?" My heart almost stopped. "What happened?" I asked, without really wanting to know. "The radio says they've been killed in a plane crash somewhere up north." I hung up without saying goodbye and started dialing Duck's number, praying he would answer. I had been at Stax the Friday before when Otis was leaving and I knew that the MGs were on the road that weekend as well. Duck's phone rang and rang, but no answer.

I sat there in disbelief, not knowing what to do. I called Cropper's house, no answer. People started calling, asking me what was going on, but I just put them off and kept dialing Duck's number. I turned my radio on to get some news of what happened, but I turned it off again, realizing I really didn't want to hear it. I called Duck for thirty minutes,

87

and was just about to lose it when after about the fifteenth call, Duck answered, out of breath. When I heard his voice, I could hardly speak.

"What happened, Duck?" I asked, almost in tears because I was so glad to hear his voice. "June picked me up at the airport and I just walked in the door," he said, getting his breath. "Otis and the Bar-Kays are dead," he told me. "All except for James Alexander and Ben Cauley. Their plane crashed somewhere in Wisconsin." You could tell it hadn't sunk in yet, 'cause Duck loved Otis. He had played on all his records and had backed him at the Monterey Pop Festival the summer before. Otis had even been to his house for Duck's birthday party that October. Although everyone had gotten drunk at the party, Otis was the only one to apologize for doing so, and now he was dead.

The radio had made a mistake. It was the Bar-Kays, not the MGs, who had been killed with Otis. This caused a lot of anxious moments for friends and relatives in Memphis for both groups. Duck and the MGs attended Otis's funeral in Macon, Georgia. He told me later it was a circus, with fans rushing James Brown and other artists who had also attended. But the worst thing that happened came two weeks later, when a UPS truck pulled up outside Stax and unloaded Carl Lee Cunningham's drums. Carl Lee had been the shoeshine boy in the barbershop next door to Stax seven years earlier. Al Jackson had spent long hours teaching him to play and he had turned out to be one of the best drummers in the country. Now he was dead and his drums, still in their cases, sat in the hallway of Stax, all warped and discolored from days under Wisconsin Bay, standing like some bizarre monument to a young life, forever nineteen.

SWEET HOME ALABAMA

In 1969, I discovered Muscle Shoals Sound Recording Studios in Sheffield, Alabama. Jim Stewart took me down to record Sid Selvidge's second album. I cannot tell you the impact this place had on me. Everything up 'til now was preschool compared to what I found in the quad cities of Sheffield, Tuscumbia, Muscle Shoals, and Florence by the Tennessee River, which flowed serenely through this beautiful valley. It was the most laid-back place I had ever been and it immediately felt like home.

The studio was a small, narrow shotgun building on the Dixie Highway that had served for years as home for a monument company that made tombstones for the graveyard directly across the street. The place bore no resemblance to its former occupant and was the most comfortable studio I had ever been in; nothing else even came close. Four musicians were partners in Muscle Shoals Sound. Jimmy Johnson managed the place and also played guitar. Roger Hawkins played drums, Barry Beckett played keyboards, and David Hood played bass. There was a surprisingly large music community there with three major studios. Rick Hall and Quinn Ivey owned the others besides Muscle Shoals Sound, which had the best musicians, the best sound, and by far the best vibes.

The talent in this small area was unbelievable. I met writers like Dan Penn, Spooner Oldham, and Donnie Fritts. I became friends with Marlin and Jeannie Green. Marlin had produced and played guitar on Percy Sledge's hit "When a Man Loves a Woman," and Jeannie did background vocals on everybody's sessions, including Elvis. They lived not far from the Tennessee River in a large volcanic rock home that Marlin had built himself. He told me he had ordered the rocks from Mexico and when they arrived by train, the man at the depot called to tell him, "Mr. Green, y'all's rocks is here," in a tone that might suggest there were some nice rocks right here in Alabama. It was a beautiful home and the finishing touch was a motorized roof over the living room. At the touch of a button, the roof slid away, revealing a starry Alabama sky. Marlin and I lay on our backs on the floor staring up at the stars while Jeannie played the baby grand piano and sang old black gospel songs with more soul than any white woman I'd ever heard.

After cutting some tracks, Duck, Bobby Manuel, and I drove back to Memphis. I hated to leave this place and promised myself I'd be back as soon as possible.

The next week I returned to California, staying with Leon and writing and recording some tracks on one of my favorite singers and guitar players, Don Preston. There had been a lot going on in the months since I had left. Leon had always kept busy arranging and producing. He had become the most sought-after arranger in Hollywood, doing sessions for everybody from Frank Sinatra to the Beach Boys. Now he was thinking about being an artist. He had the respect of anyone who knew him and most who didn't know him. One Sunday afternoon, he asked me what I thought about a big band with amplified horns, three drummers, and a fifteen-voice choir. I told him that it sounded great if he could pull it off.

I guess I forgot who I was talking to, 'cause the next Sunday afternoon we were all there, gathered together in a large rehearsal hall with over twenty people playing, singing, and having a great time. Jim Horn

The Delaney and Bonnie sessions at Stax, 1969.
Left to right: Booker T., Bonnie Bramlett, Duck
Dunn, David Porter, Al Jackson, Delaney Bramlett,
Isaac Hayes, Steve Cropper.
Photo: Don Nix.

90

led the horn section, which included some of the top session players in Hollywood. Jim Keltner, Jimmy Karstein, and Chuck Blackwell played drums. Carl Radle played bass and there were a host of guitar players, including Jessie Ed Davis, Don Preston, and Joey Cooper. Jumping John Gallie played organ while Leon played piano and sang blues versions of songs by Bob Dylan, the Beatles, and old standards like "Misty." I sang in the choir with Francine Brokey, Kay Poorboy, Delaney and Bonnie Bramlett, and anyone else who happened by. Leon had written rough arrangements for the horns while everyone else just played along.

The building almost exploded, all that great talent singing and playing their asses off for no one but each other. It was incredible. No one who was there ever felt the same again about Claude Russell Bridges, aka Leon Russell, as an artist. I think it gave him the confidence to try it on his own. The Leon Russell Electric Horn Band lasted only three weeks, three short Sunday afternoons in a hot, windowless rehearsal hall, but it was an experience no one who was present ever forgot.

Delaney and Bonnie also had their act together working small clubs in the valley, and playing to mostly biker pool players. I thought they would be the perfect act for Stax, although Stax had never signed a white act. I called Duck and asked him what he thought. He said it was a great idea and asked me to bring some tapes for Jim Stewart to listen to. Leon had recorded some demos on them and I took those and flew back to Memphis. Jim loved the tapes and offered to fly the duo to Memphis and see if a recording deal could be struck. I called Delaney with the news and they flew down a week later.

They signed on Friday afternoon and recording started the following Monday with Duck and me as producers. The Delaney and Bonnie Stax album (*Home*) was recorded in less than a week, with me being relegated to a mere spectator. Booker T. and the MGs were the backing band, Wayne Jackson and Andrew Love on horns, with background vocals by anyone who wandered into the studio, including William Bell and Bobby Whitlock. From the outset it became clear to Duck and me that Delaney was calling the shots. From the material to the way the whole thing went down, it was his show. Bonnie was no help, giving all authority to her loving husband. What could have been the album of the decade turned out to be no more than a fart in a hurricane, and although we remained friends, we never worked together again.

Paramount Records had bought Stax, and Duck and I were asked to produce Charlie Musselwhite, one of their artists. After the Delaney and Bonnie fiasco, we weren't sure about producing anyone, but we finally agreed. We started the album at Ardent, and it was a disaster from the get-go. Charlie came in with his manager and barely spoke to us. We had gotten together some songs for his consideration, but Charlie refused to listen, saying he had his own material. He brought in four black guys from Chicago who were almost good. They stayed to themselves most of the week, consuming large amounts of alcohol. The first night of recording, the bass player got so drunk he had to play sitting in a metal folding chair. In the middle of the second take of a most forgettable song, he fell over on top of his head and just lay there while Duck went out and finished the song for him. The third night, Duck didn't even show up and I finished the album alone. Charlie recorded sitting down playing harmonica and singing while his manager sat beside him in one corner of the studio, and the band played huddled together in another corner.

It's one of the strangest sessions I've ever had anything to do with, and no surprise that it produced a terrible album. So bad, in fact, that neither Duck nor I wanted anything to do with it. When we turned the album in we listed production credits as a Mike & Jeff Production, after Duck's two sons, then age seven and five. 1969 ended without a feeling of great accomplishment.

THE BIG TIME

GREAT GREAT BRITAIN
AND COPENHAGEN, TOO

ineteenseventy started with a bang. I spent New Year's Eve with Duck and his family along with Dan Penn and his wife, Linda. We all sat around telling stories and laughing. Dan relayed the tale of growing up in the small town of Vernon, Alabama. He couldn't go out for the high school football team because his father feared he might be seriously injured. Dan decided the only way to change his daddy's mind was to embarrass him and go out for the cheerleading squad instead, something unheard of for a male high school student in the '50s, especially in Vernon, Alabama.

Cheerleaders were picked by the student body at a Wednesday morning assembly program. Each candidate of the squad came on the stage alone, doing a cheer of her (in Dan's case, his) choice. When Dan's turn came, he encountered a largely amused group of applauding schoolmates. Dan was struck dumb as he took his place stage center, forgetting the cheer he had written especially for the occasion. Duck and I were in tears, rolling on the floor, trying our best to breathe. When we finally came around, Duck asked him if his daddy had given in. "Yeah, I guess he felt sorry for me, but I broke my collarbone in the last practice before the season and never even got my name on the program," he said, still disgusted with his luck, and we were on the floor again.

After Dan and Linda left, I decided to spend the night in the guest room, which I did quite often. Duck told me there was a chance the MGs might go on tour in England and Europe at the end of January and said that I might be able to go along. There were a lot of ifs in this deal, but I was so excited I couldn't go to sleep. Duck called from Stax one afternoon a week later to tell me everything was set, and we were leaving for England in two weeks. I had always wanted to visit London. Even as a kid, I fantasized about it and I couldn't believe I was finally going. As it turned out, we left a week early due to a looming air traffic controllers' strike. Duck's brother Tom lived in Houston and worked in the tower there. He had called Duck to tell him if we were going to fly anywhere we better do it the next day or it might be weeks before we would get

93

another chance. I didn't care. I had been packed for a week and we were all gathered the next morning at the Memphis airport.

We flew to New York, where we boarded a TWA 707 for the flight to London. On board were David Ruffin and Jimi Hendrix's band, Noel Redding and Mitch Mitchell. Duck, Al, Cropper, and I sat together, while Booker T., who had brought a friend of the female persuasion along, sat as far as he could away from us. It was dark and snowing like crazy as the plane lifted off and for a brief few seconds you could see the huge snowflakes engulfing Kennedy airport before we were lost in the clouds headed out over the north Atlantic for London. Nobody slept, and if anybody tried they were awakened with one of those little bottles of whiskey they serve on airplanes dangling in front of them.

The stewardesses had a small space in the very tail of the plane where they could retreat to rest up and get away from the passengers for a while. After a few drinks, Cropper found this little hiding place and took up residence. He invited everybody back and held court for the remainder of the flight. This little room also housed the little bottles of liquor, which were kept in metal drawers with locks on them. Somewhere near Greenland, the stewardesses gave up and joined the party. The metal drawers were left open and everyone helped themselves.

We landed the next morning as the sun was coming up, and every-body rushed for the baggage area to claim luggage and instruments. We wanted to get to the hotel and bed before the liquor wore off and the cotton mouth set in. No such luck. There was customs to contend with. I went through first, telling the agent I was on holiday and showing him my travelers' checks to prove I could survive in England for the next three weeks. The MGs were not so lucky. When the immigration man asked if they were there to work, Steve told him they were Booker T. and the MGs and they were there for a tour and a work permit should be on file. Everyone had forgotten that in the haste to beat the air traffic con-trollers' strike, no one had informed the English authorities that we were coming a week early.

The immigration people stood firm: Booker T and the MGs had no work permit on file and were not going to be allowed in. Everyone was asked to take a seat until everything was straightened out. I watched all of this from the other side of the immigration booth, so I went down-stairs, where by this time all our luggage was going 'round and 'round the luggage carousel. I got a cart and put everybody's instruments and bags on it, then went back upstairs to see how the customs dilemma was coming. Duck, Steve, Al, Booker, and friend were still sitting in the same small waiting area, sort of like they were in purgatory. I took a seat on the stairs, waiting for an end to this Mexican standoff. After an hour, things started happening. A new shift came on, relieving the guys who were holding my friends hostage. Duck and Steve didn't look well. They seemed to have more luggage under their eyes than they did downstairs. All at once the customs area turned into a family reunion. The new guy in charge was named Kerry Lewis, and he was the president of the Booker T. and the MGs fan club in Great Britain. Will wonders ever cease?

The tour covered the usual cities and towns in England: Manchester, Liverpool, Blackpool, Newcastle, Coventry, and, of course, London. There were actually two concerts in London, one at the start and another after the band returned from Scandinavia. I fell in love with England. You have these mental pictures of places and most of the time you are disappointed when you finally arrive, but not England. It surpassed anything I ever imagined. I went to all the museums and visited every antique shop on Kings Road. Someone took us to the Speakeasy Club on Margaret Street. It was on a weekend and the place was packed. On the next Tuesday evening, Duck, Steve, and I went back and found the place almost deserted. We sat at the bar and ordered a pitcher of beer. There were only six or eight people sitting at tables with nothing but a jukebox playing. One of those people walked over and asked, "Aren't you Steve Cropper?" When Steve replied, "Yes," the man said, "Jimi Hendrix would like to meet you," and we walked over and sat at their table for an hour of casual talk and beer drinking. I remember how surprised I was at how soft-spoken and laid-back Hendrix was, not at all like the madman he could be on stage.

The band was off for a few days, so I flew down to Paris to see friends I had met when they visited Stax on vacation in Memphis. I flew back on Sunday night and was at Heathrow again on Monday morning to fly with the MGs to Copenhagen. Damn, I felt just like a jetsetter. Denmark is probably another book on its own. We had always heard of the sexual freedom in this country, but I don't think any of us were ready for what we were about to experience. It started immediately as we were checking in to the Three Falke Center Hotel. Duck started punching me, motioning with his head toward a news rack full of magazines with the most sexually explicit covers we had ever seen.

The guy at the desk saw it all. He turned and picked up one of the porno mags, flipping quickly to the centerfold, which he held open for all to see. We just stood there frozen. He said very loudly, "You'll like this one. It's got a girl fuckin' a pig."

Since none of us had ever heard of anything like that, much less
seen pictures, we walked away quickly, got on the elevator, and went to
our rooms to mold a reply to this hawker of filthy pictures. We were all
Southern boys, brought up by churchgoing parents who would have a
heart attack if they knew things like this were being sold in full view of
their boys. I can't speak for Al and Booker, but I know for a fact that
Duck, Steve, and I had kept an old copy of *Gents* magazine hidden
somewhere in our sock drawer all through junior high, but this was
serious business. These mags could get you jail time where we were from
and everyone approached them like a possum hunt: after dark and very
slowly.

The next afternoon there was a press party where someone slipped
Duck a piece of paper with an address on it, telling him if we went there,
we'd never forget it. The name of the place was the Club Erotica, and
we figured the place must be a nightclub with a racy floor show. We
figured wrong. The place didn't open 'til about midnight and the cover
charge was substantially more than any nightclub we had ever been to.
The Club Erotica was two small rooms. The first held a well-stocked bar
and display cases full of the nastiest-looking hardware you've ever seen,
dirty books, and all kinds of salves, lotions, and creams. In the other
room we found about twenty straightback chairs surrounding a large
comforter on the floor. There were several colored spotlights in the ceiling above the comforter. Only a quarter of the chairs were full, mostly
men, but there were three or four women present.

We had been seated only a few minutes when a guy dressed in leather
wearing a mask and carrying a whip came through the door. His voice
sounded remarkably like the guy who had just taken our money out front.
With great fanfare he announced the first act of the evening. I won't go
into what took place for the next hour or so. I'll just say we were shocked,
and more than just a little put off by the whole spectacle. Everyone was
married but me, and I guess by this time in the tour everyone was ready
for some kind of release, but this was more than we had signed on for.
I guess some people found this display of demeaning behavior a turn-
on. Me, I've had bigger hard-ons at a tractor pull.

At a break in the show, Mr. S&M came over and introduced himself, but nobody wanted to shake his hand. He told us he was thinking
about taking his rude little show to America, maybe playing Las Vegas
or Reno. I thought to myself, "You try taking this nasty rig to America
and they'll tar and feather you." Of course this was twenty-five years ago;
nowadays they'd probably welcome him with open arms. I asked him

THE BIG TIME

Don Nix (left) and Al Jackson arriving
in Uppsala, Sweden.
Photo: Duck Dunn.

where the restroom was and he pointed toward a door. "Just go through
there and take a left." So I walked through the door and found myself
outside in subzero weather; to my left was a large snowbank. I'd had
about enough of this for one night and so had everybody else, so we took
a cab back to the hotel and locked our doors.

From Copenhagen we flew to Stockholm in a driving blizzard.
January is not the best time to visit Scandinavia. We traveled from Stockholm to Malmö, Göteborg, and Uppsala before returning to Stockholm.
It was snowing so hard in Malmö that we had to follow airline employees holding red umbrellas who were spaced five feet apart to find the
airplane. Once we were on board, a big truck pulled up and sprayed
deicing liquid on the drooping, snow-laden wings, and we pulled away
quickly before more snow could take its place and kill us all.

Needless to say we were glad to get back to London for one more
concert at the Odeon Hammersmith before going home. The place was
packed, as all the venues had been. To cap it off, a lot of English musicians came backstage to say hello, including two of the Rolling Stones,
Bill Wyman and my personal favorite, Charlie Watts. The next morning we arrived at Heathrow for the flight home. I remember walking
down the long concourse toward our gate. I saw the tail of a very large
airplane in the distance. As we got closer, I realized this three-story tail

section was attached to the aircraft we were about to board. While we were in Sweden, there had been the maiden flight of the Boeing 747, the largest commercial aircraft ever to fly. Our flight left at 10 A.M., but there was another New York flight at twelve o'clock on the smaller and time-tested 707. Booker and his lady friend opted for the latter. I guess a lot of people did because there were fewer than fifty people on our flight. After sweating out the takeoff (Duck allowed they'd never get it off the ground) we relaxed and had a great flight. We arrived in Memphis that night, tired and glad to be home, knowing this would not be our last trip to England.

LOOK OUT! ALBERT'S GOT A GUN

A couple of months later, I got a call from Al Jackson, who had been producing Albert King as well as overseeing his other studio duties. Al was always easygoing, but this call had a sense of urgency I had never heard from him. "Man, you've got to produce Albert King for me! He's driving me crazy." I had known Albert for about four years and he always seemed okay, but I had heard stories from producers and musicians that he could be hard to get along with. Still, I was a fan and I jumped at the chance. "When do I start?" I asked. He told me to work that out with Jim Stewart and wished me good luck. The way he said it, though, took a little of the excitement out of the moment.

I met Jim a few days later and he said he would like me to record a live album of Albert at the Fillmore West, where he was playing a month later with B. B. King, and it might be possible to get the two on tape together. It was an exciting project and I knew who I wanted for a band. I called Leon that night with the news and asked him to get in touch with the basic members of the Electric Horn Band. The plan was to hold rehearsals at Leon's Skyhill Studio for two days before flying to San Francisco for the gig. Duck and I flew to L.A. and checked into the Hyatt House on Sunset, where Albert was already staying. The next afternoon we all met at Leon's to rehearse. There were Don Preston and Joey Cooper on guitars, Chuck Blackwell and Jim Keltner on drums, Duck and Carl Radle were going to try dual basses, and John Gallie and Leon were playing keyboards. There was absolutely no better band in existence and they were all excited to be playing with Albert and the possibility of backing B. B.

Rehearsals got going and there was trouble from the start. Albert stood by the doorway as the band jammed for about fifteen minutes and

Leon Russell and Albert King,
Muscle Shoals Studios, 1971.
Photo: Don Nix.

seemed reluctant to join in. Finally, I asked him to play some and he spent another fifteen minutes tuning his guitar while everyone sat around and waited. An uneasiness settled over the studio. Finally, Albert was ready and sang and played a couple of songs before setting his guitar down and walking from the room without saying a word to anyone. I followed him to the control room and asked him what was wrong. "The band ain't groovin' man, they just ain't groovin'," he said.

I was stunned. I told him, "Albert, this is the best band around and they're lookin' forward to playing with you."

"No, man. Them drummers can't keep time and there's too many guitar players."

He said this without looking at me and I knew Albert wasn't giving me the whole story. I tried to convince him again that this could be one of the best live albums ever recorded if he would just trust me to work it out. This made him mad. I was asking him to do something against his better judgment and he was pissed. He didn't say anything, he just put his hands on his hips, pulling his coat back to reveal the black .45 pistol he always carried. I knew he wasn't going to shoot me, it was just his way of telling me the conversation was over. I was not only mad, I was embarrassed. How could I go back in to the studio and tell my friends that Albert didn't like the way they played? I left. I walked out of the house, drove back to the hotel, got my bag, and drove to the airport. I got the next plane to Memphis and went to bed. The hell with him!

I learned later that Albert never went on stage with musicians better than he was. I had seen him at clubs on several occasions and his backing bands had always been mediocre at best. It didn't matter in the studio, but live Albert King had to be the star and the best musician on stage. I think he was probably threatened by the band I had put together in California. The more I got to know him, the better I understood him. Albert could not read or write and I think this fact put him on the defensive most of his life, since he didn't want anyone to know. I remember being in the studio at Stax one day during one of his sessions. David Porter and Isaac Hayes were upstairs writing songs for Albert's album. They did that a lot. "Writin' on the run," as Jimmy Reed called it.

David ran into the studio with a legal pad with the words to a new song he and Isaac had just written. Isaac went to the piano while David gave the words to Albert. "You're going to love this," he told Albert, who not only didn't love it but stomped out of the studio while everyone sat there in disbelief. Albert didn't want anyone to know that he couldn't read, which made it kind of hard to produce records on him.

The bottom line was, Albert did not like to be upstaged, on or off the bandstand. He was the man and that was it, but he did have his softer side, as he would prove to me later.

Albert called me two weeks later and apologized for the California fiasco. Not formally, mind you, but still enough to make me forget about it. Albert sometimes reminded me of a small child, and this made it hard to stay mad at him for very long. He asked if I still wanted to produce his next album, which of course I did, but there was one stipulation. We'd do it at Muscle Shoals Sound with their musicians. Albert agreed and I booked a week, hoping to have the tracks recorded in that time and do the vocal overdubs at Stax. I had to come up with some songs, so I called Dan Penn and asked if he had any. He didn't and suggested we go somewhere quiet and write some.

So two days later we flew to San Francisco and checked into the Miyako Hotel. Duck came with us, and as we walked across the lobby to check in we ran into Jim Keltner, who was in town playing some sessions.

Albert King at Stax Studios, Memphis, 1969.
Photo: Don Nix.

ROAD STORIES AND RECIPES

We spent four nights there and had a great time and even wrote two or
three pretty good songs. Dan and I wrote a slow blues ballad called "Like
a Road Leading Home" and I wrote "Bay Area Blues" with Duck, and
pieces of two or three more.

A week later, I met Albert at the Holiday Inn in Florence, where we
spent a delightful week together recording eleven tracks for his album
Lovejoy. We even had time to overdub his vocals and guitar solos. Since I
had written eight of the songs, it seemed my hardest job would be teaching the words to Albert, who still denied the fact he couldn't read. It was
a silly game. I mean, when we went to lunch, Albert would study the
menu while I read aloud what I thought he might like. "Hmmm, that
chicken fried steak sure looks good, or I might like some of that lasagna."
You had to keep going like this 'til you hit on something he liked. Sometimes it seemed like a skit right out of *Amos and Andy.*

Finally one night, while we sat in his hotel room going over some
lyrics he was to overdub the next day, I told him, "Albert, I know you
can't read, but if I could play guitar like you I wouldn't care if I could
read or not."

He sat there looking at me for a long while. I thought for a minute
he was going to pull that big old army issue .45 out of his britches and
shoot me. A big broad grin came across his face and he stuck out his
hand. "I like you Don. You alright." I will never forget it.

The next day he went into the vocal booth and put on his head-
phones. While the playback came through one cue system, I plugged the
mike into another. As the track played I gave Albert the next line of the
song through the phones. Kind of like following the bouncing ball. He
loved this setup so much that the next day he had me put a music stand
in the vocal booth with the lyrics on it, so anyone else in the studio would
think he was reading them. It was our little secret, and that week together
in the studio made us friends for life.

The evening Martin Luther King was shot, Duck and I were standing on the sidewalk in front of Stax. We were just hanging out with some
of the neighborhood kids killing time. As word of the shooting spread,
people filled the streets and things were starting to get ugly. Duck and
I knew most of the people who were gathered at McLemore and College,
but the safety we had felt over the past seven years was gone in less than
a minute. Isaac Hayes told us to come inside and offered us a ride out
of the neighborhood in his gold-plated Cadillac, but we refused since

THE BIG TIME

we still felt safe in our own cars. As I drove out of south Memphis, I noticed smoke billowing from dozens of fires.

I don't think I realized the danger until I arrived home and turned on the TV. Walter Cronkite was on telling the world that Martin Luther King had died from the bullet through his throat and as he spoke the words I realized he was the same man who told me JFK had been murdered in Dallas. The news of King's death rocked Memphis and other cities across America, sparking riots and unrest that would change us all forever. After King's death, College and McLemore became an armed camp. Stax erected a twelve-foot cyclone fence with barbed wire coiled along the top. An electric gate allowed only artists and employees to enter, and uniformed guards patrolled the building and parking lot twenty-four hours a day.

Although I still spent most of my days in Memphis at the studio, the fun was gone. The days when all the neighbors were invited into the studio and the musicians were invited into the neighborhood were over. So was Mrs. Axton's record shop. Even she had been bought out and I think that changed things a lot around the place, and not for the better. It was now almost 1971, just ten years since the small company, with absolutely nothing, had grown into a major player in the record business. Every major label was in Memphis trying to get in on the action. All of them failed. They didn't get it. The Memphis Sound was something you couldn't capture in a jar and take back to L.A. or New York to release at a whim. It wasn't just a sound, it was people—Memphis musicians and writers—who where responsible for the whole deal. It was a way of life the people who lived it didn't even understand.

Memphis had been busting at the seams for years, waiting to be heard, and now its time to shine had come. With people like Sam Phillips, Dewey Phillips, Jim Stewart, Estelle Axton, and Willie Mitchell to guide it, the place exploded and the whole world felt the repercussions, but now it was dying. If you ask me, the day Martin Luther King was assassinated, the Memphis music scene was mortally wounded and would die a slow, agonizing death.

❉   ❉   ❉

I flew back to California, where Leon was recording Joe Cocker. He had met Joe through Denny Cordell, Cocker's manager. It seemed that Leon was just what Joe needed at this time in his career. Marathon sessions at A&M Recording Studios and Leon's Skyhill home studio had produced some dynamite tracks like "Feeling Alright" and "The Letter."

103

Joe's backing group, the Grease Band, had been having immigration problems and it seemed a seven-week tour would have to be canceled. Enter Leon and his Electric Horn Band. Plans were made for Leon's twenty-plus piece group to take over for the four-man Grease Band. It turned out to be a logistic nightmare, but somehow Denny and Leon pulled it off. Since paying everyone enough money to live on was impossible, A&M Records subsidized the tour and plans were made to record a live album as well as film some of the concerts for a movie. The tour was billed as Mad Dogs and Englishmen, with a lot more mad dogs than Englishmen. Most of the old horn band was present, including Don Preston, Chuck Blackwell, Jim Keltner, Jim Gordon, Carl Radle, and Sandy Konikoff. The soul choir could number as many as twenty people on any given night and included Kay Poorboy, Sweet Emily Smith, Donna Washburn, Rita Coolidge, and Brown Sugar herself, Claudia Linnear. Denny leased an aging superconstellation airliner to fly the group around. One flight on that plane did it for me. I had been having bad luck as far as air travel went. This combined with the Valium made the tour look like an accident waiting to happen.

MUSCLE SHOALS

All this activity somehow motivated me to record myself. I had never really thought of myself as an artist, but with the luck I'd had producing other artists, the idea grew stronger every day. It seemed half the people I'd heard on the radio couldn't sing that well anyway. Hell, I could sing just as bad as any of 'em. I holed up in my apartment trying hard to write songs for myself. It was tough since I was my own worst critic, so I started going down to Pop Tunes record shop and bringing stacks of albums home, hoping maybe I could gain some inspiration from some of them. I listened to everything from Hank Williams to Sonny Boy Williamson to Bing Crosby.

Although Nashville is only 200 miles away, the country music scene was almost nonexistent in Memphis. We didn't even have a country music radio station then and I was glad. I had always hated hillbilly music, but Hank Williams was different. To me he sang and lived with an "I don't give a damn" attitude that appealed to me. He mixed drinking, lying, and cheating songs together with gospel, and I loved his rendition of "I Saw the Light." I had been brought up in the Baptist church and my parents insisted I go until I was fifteen. The only thing that got me through all the fire and brimstone was the music, and I memorized almost every hymn in the book. The people in the small church my family attended could really sing with beautiful harmonies and a looseness that only a Southern Baptist could understand. You could sing at the top of your lungs, which I did, and no one cared.

The first song I decided to cut was "I Saw the Light." In my head I heard the song with the blues backbeat and background vocals right out of a southern church choir. I had written fifteen to twenty songs to record and had ideas for about five or six more. I had no idea what I was going to cut, but I knew without a doubt where I wanted to cut it. I called Jimmy Johnson and booked a week at Muscle Shoals Sound.

Highway 72 is an old road that runs from Memphis through northern Mississippi and Alabama. There are long stretches of nothing but farmland, forest, and kudzu. I loved it: the heat and humidity, the sharecropper shacks, and the small sleepy towns and communities . . . The South. It's as much a part of me now as it was then, only I didn't realize it at the time. Muscle Shoals is a three-hour drive from Memphis, but a world away as far as hustle and bustle goes. To say the place was slow would be an understatement. It was so slow, in fact, that it was rumored it came to a complete stop for twenty minutes in the late '50s.

I loved Muscle Shoals. The studio with its musicians and engineers were custom-made for someone as inexperienced as I was about producing records, especially on myself. The Holiday Inn was run by Mrs. Christiansen, one of the first female innkeepers in that chain of motels, and she had set aside room 137 as a two-room music suite, complete with piano, tape recorder, and manuscript paper. There was no extra charge for these amenities, which proved just how welcome the place made you feel.

We started recording at ten o'clock Monday morning and by week's end I had eight completed tracks. I could have cut twice as many, but after working with these guys for a couple of days, I started writing in the studio, something I never would have attempted in Memphis. "I Saw the Light" was the only track I cut that I had intended to do. The other seven tracks were written and recorded from the bits and pieces of ideas I had brought with me. It was the most fun I ever had. Since my guitar playing still suffered from bad management, I worked up melodies in my head and hummed them to the keyboard player, Barry Beckett, who made a numbered chart of the chord progressions. He then made copies of the chart, which he gave to bass player David Hood and drummer Roger Hawkins. I was also using Eddie Hinton and Wayne Perkins on guitars that week.

We worked from 10 A.M. 'til 2 P.M., then broke for lunch, which we ate at the Mid City Cafe in Tuscumbia. Not only was it the Trailways Bus Station, it was the best soul-food place I'd eaten in since Burkle's in Memphis. The week passed too quickly, but I still had several tracks to record to have a complete album. I don't think I really wanted to finish so quickly because it gave me a good excuse to come back soon.

I drove back to Memphis and for the next two weeks, I overdubbed my vocals on the eight tracks I had recorded. I did this at Ardent Studios with help from Ken Woodley, who got me real high and then engineered while I muddled through one vocal after another. I also did some overdubs at Dan Penn's new studio, Beautiful Sounds on Highland Avenue. I put Jay Spell on one track called "In God We Trust," the closest thing to a war-protest song I ever recorded.

> Old men sit talking in the sun, while young men dying
>   one by one,
> But have no fear there's more where they come from.
> They say that it's a must, in God we trust.

Jay played some beautiful fiddle on that song and I decided to make it the title track. I then drove back to Muscle Shoals, and in three days I finished the album, using Jeannie and Marlin Green, the Holiday Sisters, and Telma Hopkins on background vocals. I did the final mixing at Ardent with John Fry engineering. But now that the album was completed, I had no idea what I was going to do with it. I really didn't care since the whole project had given me such a great feeling of accomplishment.

I had kept in touch with the Mad Dogs and Englishmen tour almost daily. It was now in its fifth week and by the reports I had been getting things had started to slip. I decided to rejoin the group in Dallas and flew down without telling anyone I was coming. I had been romantically involved with Cynthia Barnes, a young lady from Dallas, since the sessions I had worked on with Dale Hawkins and Bruce Channel, and the trip's purpose was as much to see her as it was to see the band.

We bought tickets and went to the concert. I was shocked. It may have been Cocker's tour, but it was sure as hell Leon's show. He was a changed man, strutting up and down directing the band in an overly exaggerated P. T. Barnum style. It seemed the top hat he had started wearing on the tour had transformed him from Ichabod Crane into the true Master of Space and Time. Although Joe sang well, he seemed tired and out of sorts, while Leon was a madman and the audience loved him.

After the show I went back stage to say hello and some of the soul choir came over to visit, and we talked and smoked well into the morning. The next afternoon Leon came over and we sat around and talked for the first time in a while. You could tell he was having a good time and he seemed like a different person. I told him about the album I had just finished. He said he and Denny had planned to start a record label and for me to bring my album out after the tour. I decided to stick with the tour for a few days, but by this time morale seemed kind of low. The rehearsals five weeks before had been almost magic with everyone excited and ready to go, but now everyone seemed on edge and tired. Such is life on the road. I flew back to Memphis after a couple of days.

I had missed Furry and I drove downtown to see him, but he was gone, as was Goodkid, and no one knew where they were. I never did find Goodkid, but after a long search, I found Furry at a friend's house in midtown. He was sleeping on the couch and had all his belongings in a paper grocery bag. He wore only a t-shirt, old baggy pants, and house shoes. Once again his friends came together and rented him a small duplex at 811 Mosby, getting his guitar out of hock, and buying enough food to get him by for a while. I took Furry to Ardent studios one rainy Sunday afternoon. I turned on the tape machine and let it run for two hours. Furry sang, talked, and jived his way through this session and it was the most candid I'd ever seen him. At one point in the afternoon he came out with this poem:

Our Father who art in Washington
Nixon is his name
He took me off Bull Durham
and put me on golden grain
The sweetest flower I ever smelt
was Lilly of the beach
The worst whiskey I drank in my life
was right here on Leath Street
The hoppa grass makes the hop
and the honey bee makes the honey
The good Lord makes all the pretty girls
and Sears and Roebuck makes the money
Thank you

I was floored. The next day I edited the poem and inserted it into "Iuka," the last song on my album.

The first week in June, I flew to L.A. and moved into a house in Sherman Oaks that Denny Cordell had rented for Joe and himself. Cocker was in terrible shape. Not only was he exhausted, he never ate. He lay in the living room on a beanbag smoking hash all day. He seldom spoke and he seemed in a constant state of depression and even confusion.

One evening we got a call from a friend who had visited the house on several occasions. She had been busted at Bullocks for shoplifting a belt and the police were holding her at the Van Nuys station. She wanted me and Joe to bail her out. I remember thinking to myself, "This poor thing must be in a lot of trouble to call us for help." But the dilemma gave Joe new purpose to life, and he insisted we call a cab to take us to the nearest bail bonds company. We explained our plight to the taxi driver, who took us to a seedy part of downtown L.A. where all the bail

110

Don Nix and Joe Cocker, Hollywood, 1971.

companies were located. Finding the first two or three closed, we finally ended up in a dingy office staffed by a short, wiry Mexican lady who spoke little English. She spoke even less English when she learned that Joe wanted to write her a check for the young lady's bail.

I tried the best I could to explain that this wasn't just any old check, but one from Joe Cocker himself. She took the check and looked at it for about thirty seconds. I asked, "You have heard of Joe Cocker, haven't you?" She hadn't. I was glad we had the cab wait.

But Joe wasn't giving up. He was going to get this girl out of jail that night if it short-dicked every pygmy in the Congo. He explained to the lady that he had been the recipient of several gold records and had thousands, if not millions, stashed in the bank somewhere in his name. She was a tough sale. Joe stood there in the dimly lit office barefoot and wearing the same tie-dyed shirt and jeans he had worn on the Mad Dogs tour. His hair looked like crows had been nesting in it. The little woman took a long pull on her unfiltered king-size cigarette and slowly exhaled a fog bank into the cramped quarters.

She cocked one eye at Joe. "You got gold records? Show me gold records."

We jumped back into the cab and after the long ride back to Sherman Oaks we found a gold album in a box of junk. The glass had been broken but we took it back downtown, where we found the little Mexican lady standing in the same spot we had left her in an hour before. Joe presented her the gold album with the look of triumph on his face.

She looked at the album and then at Joe, then at the album, and back at Joe again. "Who's your boss?" she asked, which startled Joe. He didn't know who his boss was, or even if he was supposed to have one. He finally blurted out "Herb Albert!" who was the president of A&M Records, Joe's label at the time.

A look of recognition crossed the lady's face and she squealed, "And the Teeeee-a-juana Brass!" "The very same," Joe acknowledged. She was almost ready to take Joe's check, but not quite. She asked Joe if he had Herb's home phone number, which, to my surprise, Joe spouted off the top of his head. The cheerful lady dialed the number and, after several rings, Herb Albert himself answered. By this time it was well past midnight and I'm sure he was asleep, but he assured the lady that Joe Cocker's check would be good for any amount he wished to write it for. That did it, and after writing a check and signing some papers, we were off back to the valley to free the young prisoner, who was glad to be out of jail.

111

Joe came back to the house and settled down on his beanbag like a king on his throne. For the next few days a slight smile curled the corners of his lips. Joe Cocker, friend to many, hero to all.

GIMME SHELTER

Denny had rented an old run-down house on the wrong end of Hollywood Boulevard across from a porn theater. The record company that he and Leon formed was called Shelter, and Denny bought my album. Although Leon wanted me to record it again in California, it was finally decided it would be released as it was. It was not your usual Hollywood record company. It had a casual atmosphere without the intimidating bullshit that prevailed at other labels. Everyone was welcome and everyone came; it seemed like a dream come true and it almost was.

For anyone who remembers the artist-signing photos on the first few pages of *Cashbox* and *Billboard* magazines in the '60s and '70s, mine was a bit different. Most artists were photographed sitting between smiling, bearded, overweight record execs, producers, and attorneys with bad combovers. My picture was taken in the front yard of Shelter while I changed a flat tire on Leon's rundown '61 Thunderbird with one hand and signed my contract with the other. Leon had purchased a pinstriped, double-breasted gangster suit that morning especially for the occasion, and stood poised against the open door of the T-bird with mirrored sunglasses and a long stogie in his mouth. Denny was sitting by the rear of the car holding a gun on me with one hand and holding a *National Enquirer* in the other. The headline read, "Bomber Pilots High on Drugs Could Trigger Nuclear Holocaust." There was a bottle of Ripple wine sitting on the ground beside him and a joint hanging from his lips. The weird thing was, the trade mags actually ran the photo with the caption we had written: "Don Nix takes time out from his whirlwind cross country tour to sign his new contract with Shelter Records. Flanking the Memphis Lark are V.P. Leon Russell (standing) and label prexy, Denny Cordell." No sir, not your everyday record company.

Since our albums were to be released simultaneously, it was decided I would perform with Leon on an upcoming TV special. Leon had persuaded the people in charge to let him produce the show. He basically wanted to tape a six-hour concert in the studio and edit it down to an hour. A week before the taping we were sitting around Shelter going over what we wanted to do on the show. My album was playing in another room, and when Furry came on with his "Hoppa Grass Makes the

The famous signing photo, Hollywood, 1970.

Hop" poem, Leon jumped up. "That's who we need. Furry Lewis. Let's get him out here for the show." Everyone agreed, and I was on the next flight to Memphis to find Furry and get his guitar out of hock and talk him into flying to California.

Finding Furry was easy. So was getting his guitar from the pawn shop, but talking him into getting on an airplane was another story. He confided in me that it wasn't so much flying that bothered him as it was the fear of dying away from home. He told me, "I just don't want to get off somewhere and die." It was a hard point to argue since there was no guarantee I could make that he would return in one piece. Furry had one leg, he was 73 years old, he chain smoked and drank anything available at all hours of the night and day. I was amazed he had made it this far.

I called Denny and Leon and told them of Furry's reluctance to visit California. Denny made him an offer he couldn't refuse. I don't

Don Nix, Furry Lewis, Sweet Emily Smith,
and Leon Russell, Los Angeles, 1970.
Photo: Jimmy Chappell.

remember how much money Shelter paid Furry, but it was enough to overcome whatever fears he had about the trip. Two things Furry insisted on: Number one, a round-trip ticket. He wanted to make damn sure he wouldn't be stuck in some Godforsaken place like California. Number two, I had to fly with him both out and back. If he was going to risk both life and limb on an airplane, then I should be willing to do the same.

We were to leave at 9:30 in the morning on a nonstop flight to L.A., so I spent the night with him so we could get an early start. We stopped at my parents' house to eat breakfast since it was on the way to the airport. My dad really liked Furry and tried to reassure him about the safety of flying, although the highest my dad had been off the ground was on a ladder to paint the house. Furry was too nervous to eat, and as we walked to the car my dad called out, "Don't worry Furry, those planes never crash." Furry turned around, "Yeah, but there's a first Sunday in every month." He was starting to make me nervous.

On the way to the airport, Furry asked me to stop at a liquor store where he had me buy him a pint of whiskey and a jar of pickled pigs' feet. I told him, "Furry, it's eight o'clock in the morning!" "Yeah, and ain't it a beautiful morning!" he said. He ate the pigs' feet by the time we got to the airport and boarded the flight, as well as drinking half the whiskey. As we walked down the jetway, Furry asked me what airline we were flying. I told him, and as we entered the aircraft a smiling stewardess waited to greet us. Furry said in a loud voice, "American Airlines is the smoovvvest airlines in the whole world," as if in doing so he guaranteed himself and everyone else aboard a safe flight. The crew was startled to say the least, and they kept a keen eye on me and Furry all the way to L.A.

The flight was uneventful and we arrived in one piece, much to Furry's dismay. The TV show was nothing more than a good ol' Leon Russell jam session with him singing not only songs from his new album, but songs from everyone else's albums. I did some songs from my new album and Claudia Linnear, Kathy McDonald, and Jim Horn did solo spots, and we found out just how hard it was to fill up six hours with continuous music. It was the first national appearance of Leon's band, the Shelter People, with most of the Mad Dogs backing band in attendance. Don Preston and Joey Cooper played guitars, Chuck Blackwell drums, Johnny Gallie on organ and Fender Rhodes keyboard bass, with Claudia and Kathy singing background vocals. It was without a doubt the best band west of the Mississippi.

Furry and I had arrived in L.A. two days before the show, and from the minute we landed he wanted to go home. He missed his house, his friends, and Memphis in general. I tried my best to console him, but I had my work cut out for me. He stayed at the house with Denny, Joe, and me, and I spent most of my time trying to convince him that everything was going to be all right. He would look at Joe and ask me, "What's that man smoking?" I started feeling bad about bringing him out and promised I would take him home as soon as the TV show was over. During the show, Furry sat in a rocking chair sipping whiskey, while sweet Emily Smith baked a cake beside him. He sat there for five hours and then it was his turn. I had heard Furry sing and play for years, but that day was the first and only time I heard him sing with a full band.

The last song of the show found Furry and Leon on the piano bench, with Leon playing and Furry singing. He was singing about going home, and at one point he stood up in front of the piano bench and grabbed his coat by the lapels. Everyone thought he was going to take his coat off, but he just wanted to show everybody the American Airlines ticket he had in his inside coat pocket. As soon as the show was over, I took Furry to the airport, where we waited for four hours for the next flight to Memphis. Furry was glad to get home and so was I.

HELP, CHUCK, HELP!

In August, Leon booked a week at Muscle Shoals Sound to record tracks for his second album. He arrived with his full band and entourage, including Sweet Emily Smith as chief cook and bouncer. They rented a house on the river just north of town and set up commune-style to eat, sleep, and play together. There was a long pier jutting into the river and everybody bought fishing gear and stood on the dock smoking dope and fishing for catfish. There was a small rowboat, which Don Preston and Joey Cooper favored over the pier since they fancied themselves big-time anglers. Everyone partied and fished for a couple of days before going in to record.

Leon set up concert-style in the small studio with monitor speakers in every corner. Everything went down live and the little building

Don Nix, Don Preston, Claudia Linnear, Kathy McDonald, Furry Lewis, and Leon Russell filming their TV special, Los Angeles, 1970.
Photo: Jimmy Chappell.

THE BIG TIME

almost shook off its foundation. No one had ever seen that much energy released in such a small space before and that, mixed with some strange pills Kay Poorboy had flown in from New Orleans, made it almost more than one could stand. The only trouble with this recording technique was the emotional and physical drain it placed on everyone. The sessions usually ended before 10 P.M., when everyone returned to the river house for some relaxation and midnight fishing.

On the third night, Leon, Chuck, and I were in lawn chairs on the dock with our lines in the water, while Don and Joey took the rowboat out to mid-river. There was also a boat with an outboard motor pulled up on the bank, which the owner of the house had locked to keep some crazed musician from running amok in it. But the lock was no match for the nimble fingers of Jumpin' John Gallie, and he and Chuck had taken the boat to town a couple of times. Everything was quiet and the night was as black as Egypt when all at once the stillness was interrupted by a loud splash from the dark river. We found out later that Don Preston, who is not a small person, got a call from nature and a nibble on his line about the same time. He didn't want to return to the house, so he dropped his pants, stuck his big ol' white butt over the side of the boat, pulled a joint out of his shirt pocket, and settled back for a good ol' country dump. Trouble was, he settled back too far and the small boat rolled over, throwing the two pro-sport fishermen with all their gear into the cold, dark water.

After the splash, panicked cries of "Help, Chuck, Help!" echoed over the river while we sat there in disbelief. The first thing that crossed my mind was why would anybody in any kind of danger call Chuck Blackwell for help. I mean, I love Chuck and always have, but in those days he was not the person you wanted to send for ammunition. But that night, Chuck rose to the occasion, ran down the pier to the motor boat, and sped into the night, rescuing Don and Joey from certain death, or almost certain death, for Don Preston still had the joint held tightly in his fist as dry as toast, which gave you an idea of where his priorities lay.

117

PALACE OF THE KING

In the fall of 1970, Denny Cordell called me and asked if I would be interested in producing Freddie King with Leon. Denny had just signed Freddie to Shelter and wanted me to coproduce him. I had been a fan of Freddie's for years, ever since I had heard "Hideaway," the greatest instrumental recorded since "Honkytonk." I jumped at the chance, and

Leon Russell, Duck Dunn, Freddie King, and
Don Nix at Chess Studios, Chicago, 1970.
Photo: Ed Caraeff.

Denny told me to meet Leon in October in Denver, where he would be
on tour.

I flew to Denver carrying a Delvacchio Dobro that Leon wanted to
use on the session. As I waited for my luggage, I realized the Dobro was
not forthcoming. I walked down to customer service and inquired about
the guitar. I was taken back to the luggage department and shown a cardboard box containing an unrecognizable stringed instrument. It seemed
the Dobro came down the conveyor belt first and was laid aside to be
placed on top of the luggage in the cart. However, it was forgotten on
the tarmac, and as the plane was pushed back for the continuing flight,
it was run over by the Braniff 727. It gave a whole new meaning to flat-
wound strings.

I stayed with Leon for a few days, writing songs for the session, which
was to be recorded at Chess Studios in Chicago. We wrote "Palace of the

King" and "Living on the Highway" and prayed that Freddie would like them. Neither of us had ever met Freddie and were intimidated at the thought of getting to record with him. We flew to Chicago, spent a restless night, and went to the studio the next day not knowing what to expect. We entered the Chess building and took the elevator to the studios—just walking down the halls of that building gave me chills. These were the same halls walked by Muddy Waters, Howlin' Wolf, Sonny Boy Williamson, and many other great bluesmen. We walked into the studio

Freddie King at Chess Studios, 1970.
Photo: Don Nix.

where they had all recorded, and you could almost feel their presence. This was mecca, the true home of the blues.

We walked into the control room and there he sat, Freddie King, the man himself. We stood there staring at each other for about two or three seconds, and my mind flashed back to my brother and me sneaking my radio under the bedcovers and listening to "Hideaway" on Dewey Phillips' *Red Hot and Blue* show. Freddie was a big man with a smile to match that immediately put us at ease. Leon and I realized we were in for a once-in-a-lifetime experience. The backing musicians on the album were basically the Shelter people, along with Duck Dunn on bass and Freddie's drummer, Charlie Myers. Chess Studios had seen little renovation since it opened. The old sound was still intact and Malcolm, the engineer, loved telling us stories of the old days.

Leon, Freddie, and I sat around the piano in metal folding chairs and went over songs for the sessions. One of the them was the tune Leon and I had written especially for Freddie, "Palace of the King," but we weren't sure if one of the verses might not offend him.

They wanted me in Russia, but Moscow was much too cold
I could have played in Denmark, but the girls are way too old.
The Italians talk funny, I don't know what they say
I can't find a chitlin' pizza for any price I pay
So I'm going back to Dallas, living in the palace of the king

The chitlin' line knocked Freddie off his chair. He loved it and wanted to record it first. We worked Monday through Thursday every day into the night, stopping only to order fried chicken from Fat Jack's, which we ate at a long table in the small dining room, listening to Freddie tell stories of the old Chess days. We hadn't realized that Freddie had played rhythm guitar on a lot of the Howlin' Wolf and Muddy Waters sessions. Freddie was a Howlin' Wolf fan and even did an impersonation of him on the fade of "Living on the Highway." The week passed way too quickly. We took the tapes to Dan Penn's studio in Memphis to overdub background vocals and percussion. We were only in the studio for a couple of days and it was over.

I said goodbye to Freddie and told him I came to Dallas every now and again and asked him for his phone number. "I'm in the book," he said, "Just look me up and give me a call the next time you're down." I was almost to the door when Freddie called out, "Hey! There's two Freddie Kings in the phone book. If you get the other one, hang up: He's a murderer."

STRANGE JAM

It was almost Christmas. I was asleep in my warm, one-room flat on Poplar Avenue. There had been light snow all day as I sat trying to write songs for my second album. The phone rang. It was Leon. "Can you come to New York right away? I need you."

I looked at the clock and it was 3 A.M. "What's wrong?" I asked. I knew he was in New York to play the Fillmore for three days.

"I fell on the street today and cracked a couple of ribs and I need you to come up and take care of me."

It might seem like a strange request for anyone who didn't know Leon, but I knew what I had to do. "I'll be there by ten o'clock," I told him. I got out of bed, packed a few things, and called the airlines. There was a flight leaving Memphis at four o'clock for New York with intermediate stops in Nashville, Washington, and Baltimore, and I was on it. I would have done almost anything for Leon, short of killing someone. He had given me a place to live in California and taught me anything I knew about writing songs or making records; I felt a loyalty to him that I've never felt for another human being. I was at the door of his hotel room at precisely ten o'clock the next morning.

Of course there was nothing I could do for Leon, he just wanted some company. Our albums had been out for a while and, although mine had received great reviews in all the right magazines, sales were not what you would call brisk. Leon's, however, had gone through the roof, and he had stayed on the road promoting it. Leon, whether he admits it or not, had always wanted to be famous and now that he was getting his wish, he was finding out it was not all it was cracked up to be. He didn't hang out much with the band. Don Preston, Joey Cooper, and Chuck Blackwell stuck together and went out shopping and sightseeing; Claudia Linnear and Kathy McDonald did the same. John Gallie stayed in his room doing God knows what, while Leon sat, smoked dope, and watched "The Price Is Right." So here I was, the court jester, fetched to do his best to cheer up the Master of Space and Time. It didn't work. By the next day I had to call in reinforcements. Duck Dunn arrived the next morning and his presence seemed to do the trick. Anyway, it was a good excuse to hang out in New York City.

On Friday night, Leon opened at the Fillmore with Elton John as the opening act. We had seen Elton a year before in a small club in L.A. at which time Leon described him as a cocktail piano player. That might have been true a year ago, but Elton had been practicing. He came out and destroyed the place with his three-piece group, including Dee

Leon Russell and Elton John, New York, 1971.
Photo: Don Nix.

Murray on bass and Nigel Olsen on drums. They were fantastic, and
Leon's mood didn't get any better as he stood in the wings and watched.
But the crowd had come to see Leon Russell and I never heard him sound
better. As soon as he walked on stage, Elton John was forgotten and it
was Leon's night.

Before the show that night, there was talk that Bob Dylan would
attend the concert. After the first show, someone came into the dressing room to tell Leon that indeed Mr. Dylan was there and would like
to come in and say hello. Everyone was excited, especially since Bob
hadn't been seen in a while because of his motorcycle accident. The band
was sitting in a circle on the floor drinking champagne when Bob and
his entourage strode in, including Robbie Robertson and Levon Helm.
Leon, Duck, and I stood in a circle talking with the three when Leon
leaned over and asked me to get my camera, which was in a drawer in the
dressing table.

THE BIG TIME

I walked over, got the camera, and walked back to the group, who were standing in a far corner of the room. As I approached, I lifted the camera to take a group shot when Dylan spotted me out of the corner of his eye. He carried an umbrella with a long silver point, which he used as a walking stick, and all at once, in a loud voice you would not expect from one so hip, he yelled, "HEY!" and tried to stab me in the face with the tip of the umbrella. I ducked just as the silver tip whizzed past my head. I stood welded to the spot as the room fell silent. I was humiliated and didn't know whether to shit or go blind, when Claudia Linnear came to my rescue. She stood up and stuck her beautiful butt toward me and said in a loud voice, "Fuck Bob Dylan, honey! You can take my picture!" With that, Bob strode out of the room. Leon looked at me with a big grin. "Don't look now, but I think we've been showtimed," he said as the whole room broke into laughter.

Duck had played some sessions in Memphis with Paul Simon at Sam Phillips' Recording Studios. Paul had given Duck his phone number in New York and told him to call when he was in town. So Duck called the next afternoon and told Paul he was in town with Leon. He asked Duck to bring Leon by if he got a chance and maybe the two of them could jam. The next evening after Leon's last show, Duck, Leon, Claudia, and I stood on a street corner in the snow trying to hail a cab uptown for a midnight jam with Paul. Finally, a cab picked us up. It was driven by a long-haired young man who didn't speak a word the whole trip, although I'm sure he recognized Leon. We had only traveled two or three blocks when he reached into his coat and pulled out a joint, which he lit up and passed around. All this in complete silence. And they say New York is not a friendly town.

We arrived at Paul's after midnight and were shown into the music room, where Simon sat playing a beautiful classical guitar. He told us the house once belonged to Andrés Segovia and this had been his music room. He showed us a couple of carved music stands that Segovia had left behind. It was all quite impressive, but there was no time for idle chit-chat. Simon handed a guitar to Leon and the two of them sat facing each other playing licks, trying to find a common denominator. It turned out that their only common ground was they both spoke English and they were each holding a guitar.

Claudia, Duck, and I sat side by side on a small sofa feeling a bit like the Three Stooges at a funeral. The more the two searched for something to play together, the more uncomfortable it became. At one point, Claudia leaned over and whispered, "Let's go find that cab driver with

123

the dope cigarettes. He was a lot more fun than this." The trouble was, Leon was high and Paul wasn't and the whole evening turned out to be a wash. Simon was nice, though, and he even called a limo to take us back to the hotel. I think he probably felt sorry for us and didn't want to see us on the street at that time of morning walking around giggling. Come to think of it, I didn't either, since we would have probably been either mugged or arrested.

CHUCK AND THE MONKEY WOMAN

In January 1971, Leon toured Europe and I went along, if for no other reason than to visit England again. On the flight from L.A. to London, Chuck Blackwell met a young lady, as he always did, who was on her way to meet her husband, who was a member of the group Iron Butterfly. The two of them talked a while in the airport, then sat together in the rear of the 707 for the flight.

Chuck always had a little medicine to help him along on these long flights, this one being eleven hours over the pole. It was a night flight and the two had some cocktails as well as a few pills that Chuck carried loose in his coat pocket. By the time the plane was over the Arctic and everyone else aboard was enjoying the Northern Lights, Chuck and his new friend dispensed with the formalities and pulled off naked. They were going at it so strong that they fogged up half the windows in the plane. The stewardesses tried their best to make them quit it, but to no avail. They reported the happenings to the pilot, who wanted no part of it, although he did make a short-arm inspection a few minutes later.

One stewardess started asking members of the band to intervene, which caused Leon to upgrade to first class, at great cost to him monetarily, but cheap at twice the price if it saved him the embarrassment of having to pull Charles Blackwell off the Monkey Woman. The best anyone could do was to keep them covered with blankets for the remainder of the trip. The next morning at Heathrow Airport, the young lady was unable to disembark under her own power. Chuck, knowing a good thing when he saw one, fetched a wheelchair and loaded her on. He was not in the best of shape either as he made a slow zigzag journey down the long corridors from the gate to customs. The Monkey Woman kept sliding out of the chair into a pile on the floor; each time, Chuck picked her up and placed her limp body back in the chair. She was completely unconscious. The befuddled passengers arriving on other flights cut a wide berth around the slow-moving, haggard couple.

Leon Russell in New York, 1971.
Photo: Don Nix.

Chuck Blackwell and Don Nix, Chicago, 1970.
Photo: Ed Caraeff.

THE BIG TIME

At immigration, a doctor was summoned to see if the young lady was well enough to enter Great Britain. An elderly man finally arrived sporting an ear trumpet, a kind of saxophone-looking gadget he held to his ear in order to better hear people's excuses for passing out on airplanes over the ocean. He questioned Chuck about what the young lady had ingested to render her so lifeless. Chuck assured the doc that she had neither injected nor swallowed anything of an illegal nature and that she was just tired from the long flight. While speaking to the doc in that slurred tone that only downers can produce, Chuck kept trying to grab the bell of his deaf aid while talking as loudly as possible.

It was decided that the young lady would have to stay in the airport infirmary until she could travel under her own power. Chuck protested this decision, and by this time had a firm grip on the hearing aid while the old man played tug-of-war with him. The immigration agents grabbed Chuck for a shakedown to see if they could find evidence of what was causing such erratic behavior. Chuck always made sure never to carry more than he could swallow on a flight, but one of the customs guys found half of a benny pill in the fuzz of his jacket pocket. Holding the pill in the middle of his palm, the guy confronted Chuck. "Young man, do you know what this is?" he asked in a stern voice as Chuck tried to focus on the tiny tablet. He finally locked in on it as a foggy smile of recognition spread across his face. "Yeah!" he said, grabbing the pill and swallowing the evidence before anyone could stop him.

We all checked in to the White House, a semi-comfortable residence hotel in Regents Park. Chuck, though on the brink of passing out all day, phoned the airport infirmary every ten minutes until they agreed to let the Monkey Woman go later that afternoon. Chuck took a taxi to fetch her and for the next two weeks she played keep-away with her husband, who was on tour in Germany and France, with excuses like "lost passport," "lost luggage," "the flu," and anything else she could think of to stay with Chuck. The poor guy fell for all of it, In-a-Gadda-Da-Vida.

Leon's first gig was the Albert Hall. I sat in the peanut gallery behind the stage with Bobby Keys and Jim Gordon. It was by far the best concert I've ever seen him play and one of the best I've ever seen, period. It was the first gig with Carl Radle on bass, which left John Gallie free to play with both hands. He had previously played keyboard bass with his left hand, and was now free to jump as high as he pleased. He jumped so hard and so high that night that Leon had to stare him down a couple of times during the two-and-a-half hour performance.

I decided not to go on the shows Leon performed on the continent, but stayed in England and bought a 1961 Rolls Royce Silver Cloud II. It wasn't something I had planned to do, it just turned out that way. I had read in the paper that morning that Prince Ali Kahn's London estate was being sold and decided to go out and look around. The estate had several Rolls and one of them caught my eye. At the end of the day, I drove the Rolls back to the hotel after paying only £5500 for it. I had never been much of a car person, but the Rolls was beautiful and the Valium and the cognac kept whispering, "Buy it. Go on and buy it." I had no idea what I was going to do with it. It was the ultimate impulse purchase.

I parked it in a no-parking zone in front of the hotel, where it sat for weeks. Every morning I went out and looked it over and never once found a parking ticket on the windshield. The hotel had a doorman named Bill who wore a top hat and tails and, because of the Rolls, he and I became friends. I learned later that it was he who kept the traffic tickets off the car. I also found out later that, for a small charge, he allowed people to sit in the Rolls under his close supervision. I had given him a key in case of some unseen emergency. He took this responsibility seriously, and one morning woke me to ask if I was interested in selling the Rolls.

It seemed that a member of the Japanese Embassy was also staying at the hotel and wanted to buy my car. I got out of bed, dressed, and went downstairs, where I found the small Oriental bouncing up and down on the seats while Bill stood guard on the curb in his top hat and tails, arms folded officially across his chest, making damn sure the little "nip" didn't try anything funny. It was worth being awakened for. I started laughing so hard, I had to step back inside the hotel until I regained my composure. The guy offered me almost twice what I paid for the Rolls, but in the end I decided not to sell.

Leon and the band returned to the U.S., but I stayed on at the White House, where Bill the doorman and I became running buddies. He seemed all right on his 7 A.M. to 2 P.M. doorman job, but after two he turned into a somewhat different person. Bill was in his late 50s. Every day when he got off work, we went around the corner to the Queenshead and Artichoke Pub, where I had a lunch of Shepherd Pie while Bill got plastered on three or four boilermakers, a double scotch mixed with a pint of beer. He then proceeded to tell me about his experiences in

World War II. He told me he was a commando and he crawled around the floor of the pub with a butter knife between his teeth, cutting the throats of make-believe Nazis between the tables. The people who owned the pub never said a word, as if they had seen these wartime maneuvers many times before.

About mid-afternoon we took the underground to Regents Street and visited the high-class travel agencies, where Bill inquired about trips to Italy, Spain, and South America. We left these agencies with stacks of brochures and printouts of price quotes for trips we would never take. We went to museums, where he gave guided tours to unsuspecting tourists. Bill still wore his top hat and tails and took great amusement from these jaunts. He was one of the craziest people I've ever met and I've always wondered what became of him.

After a couple of weeks of this, I flew to Paris to visit my friends there. I stayed there before traveling to Germany, Belgium, and finally ending up in Amsterdam, which was an adult dose. I stayed there for several days before returning to Paris, where I met a guy who offered to pick up the Rolls in London and have it shipped to New Orleans for a nominal fee. I flew back to Memphis in March to my old apartment and kept writing songs for an album that I thought "may or may not happen."

129

DRIVING SOLO

THE ALABAMA STATE TROUPERS

ne of the reviews of my album had referred to me as another one of Leon Russell's tambourine-shaking buddies and, no matter how much I disliked the remark, I knew it was dead right. I also knew that, no matter how much I loved Leon, there was no future for me at Shelter. I flew to California and played the new album I had just finished at Muscle Shoals for Denny. He said he liked the record and would pay me the same front money he had paid for the first or he would give me back my contract with no hard feelings. He understood how I felt, and when I asked for my contract back, he hugged me, wished me luck, and I flew back to Memphis.

Leon was on the road and when he heard the news he got really mad. He took my leaving as a betrayal rather than a career move and it ended our friendship. Looking back, if I had known my leaving would affect him that way, I would have probably stayed, but the damage was done and a month later I flew to New York and signed with Elektra Records.

I've never trusted music lawyers, or lawyers in general. I'd never hired one. As far as I was concerned Furry Lewis was my advisor in contractual matters regarding music. His advice was simple. Get all the money you can up front 'cause you probably won't ever see another dime. Elektra paid me $35,000 for my album, plus a subsidized tour to promote it once it had been released. I had produced an album for Jeannie Green, and she too signed with Elektra. Our albums were set to come out in June of '71 and she would join me on the promotional tour. Her husband, Marlin, had just completed an album for Lonnie Mack, who was also at Elektra. He was added to the tour.

I had met Lonnie in California a year before and we had written some songs together, which appeared on his new album. I liked Lonnie and had admired his guitar playing since his early '60s hits, "Memphis" and "Wham." Elektra had left it to me as far as picking a backing band and I went to work getting together some of the best players in Memphis and Muscle Shoals. From Memphis I asked my friend Ken Woodley to play keyboards, and Tarp Tarrant (who had played thirteen years with

Jerry Lee Lewis) to play drums. From Muscle Shoals I got Clayton Ivey on keyboards, Bob Wray on bass, and Wayne Perkins and Tippy Armstrong on guitars. I also added a second drummer, Fred Prouty, who was the staff drummer at Rick Hall's Studio. For background vocals, there was Brenda Patterson from Memphis as well as a singing group called The Minutes. It was a hell of a band.

Two weeks before the start of the tour, we were to rehearse in Muscle Shoals. Quinn Ivey and Widget Studios had offered their studios as rehearsal halls. Tarp, Ken, Brenda, and I met at the Memphis airport on a Monday morning for the one-hour flight to Muscle Shoals. We boarded an ancient Southern Airlines Martin 440, which was a two-engine propeller plane from the 1940s. As I have said, airline travel had been getting weird for me, but for some reason I liked Southern Airlines and had always trusted them to get me where I was going safely. Ken Woodley was sitting next to the window as we took off and the drone of the piston-driven engines quickly put me to sleep.

I was sleeping pretty good when I was awakened by someone shouting, "Oh shit, oh shit, oh shit!" I woke with a start and for some reason looked out the window at the engine, which seemed to be purring like a kitten. Ken, who is very soft spoken, said, "That engine's O.K., but you might want to check the other one." I looked across the aisle at the left engine, which was sitting there, still as death, cutting through the low clouds.

I looked around to see where the yelling was coming from two rows back. It was Tarp, who had completely lost it. The lone stewardess came down the aisle passing out pillows. She was very pale. She tried to give Tarp a pillow. "Fuck a pillow!" he said in panic. "Get me down!"

The stewardess disappeared into the cockpit and did not return. As the plane started a slow turn, the pilot informed us that due to the lack of emergency equipment in Muscle Shoals, we were returning to Memphis. We would land in about an hour. This news sent my pucker factor to an all-time high as we sat there like sheep being led to slaughter, losing altitude over northern Mississippi. Tarp had to be physically restrained throughout most of the flight, but as we neared Memphis he seemed to calm down a little. By the time we reached the airport, everyone on board was fried from the feeling of utter helplessness of hanging up there on one puny engine, but we finally landed. I was shocked to find fire trucks lining the runway with water cannons at the ready.

We walked down the stairway from the end of the plane and right up the ass end of another one and fifteen minutes later we were airborne

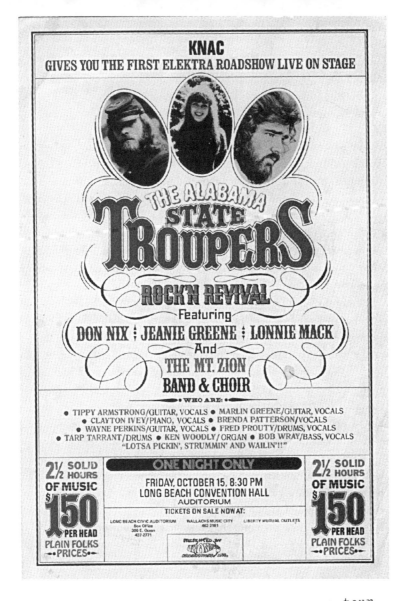

KNAC
GIVES YOU THE FIRST ELEKTRA ROADSHOW LIVE ON STAGE

THE ALABAMA
STATE
TROUPERS

ROCK'N REVIVAL
Featuring
DON NIX : JEANIE GREENE : LONNIE MACK
And
THE MT. ZION
BAND & CHOIR
• WHO ARE: •

• TIPPY ARMSTRONG/GUITAR, VOCALS • MARLIN GREENE/GUITAR, VOCALS
• CLAYTON IVEY/PIANO, VOCALS • BRENDA PATTERSON/VOCALS
• WAYNE PERKINS/GUITAR, VOCALS • FRED PROUTY/DRUMS, VOCALS
• TARP TARRANT/DRUMS • KEN WOODLY/ORGAN • BOB WRAY/BASS, VOCALS
"LOTSA PICKIN', STRUMMIN' AND WAILIN'!!"

2½ SOLID HOURS OF MUSIC $150 PER HEAD PLAIN FOLKS PRICES

ONE NIGHT ONLY
FRIDAY, OCTOBER 15, 8:30 PM
LONG BEACH CONVENTION HALL
AUDITORIUM
TICKETS ON SALE NOW AT:
LONG BEACH CIVIC AUDITORIUM   WALLACHS MUSIC CITY   LIBERTY MUTUAL OUTLETS
Box Office   462-2181
300 E. Ocean
437-2771

2½ SOLID HOURS OF MUSIC $150 PER HEAD PLAIN FOLKS PRICES

Handbill for the Alabama State Troupers tour.

again. As we reached our cruising altitude, Brenda Patterson leaned over and said, "Twenty minutes ago I swore to myself that I would never get back on one of these things and here I am. I can't believe it. Oh shit, oh shit, oh shit!"

We stayed at the Holiday Inn, which also housed that week Sam and Dave, the Staple Singers, and Aretha Franklin. Muscle Shoals had become the hub of the R&B recording industry, especially since Stax had recently lost two of its top writers and producers, Steve Cropper and Booker T. Jones. Now almost all the Stax artists recorded in Muscle Shoals.

After three days of rehearsal, Elektra sent a photographer down to take some publicity photos for the tour. We all drove out into the country and posed for one shot in front of an old black Baptist Church. The name on the cornerstone read "The Mount Zion Middle Baptist Church," and we decided to call ourselves the Alabama State Troupers with the Mount Zion Band and Choir. Things seemed to be coming together quite nicely, that is until four o'clock the next morning, when Lonnie Mack woke me from a sound sleep by beating on my door. I was still half asleep when I let him in.

"I'm leaving," he said. "I'm not supposed to be here."

I woke up real fast. "What do you mean you're leaving?" I asked.

"I'm going home. My car is already packed," and with that he was gone. He had been acting a little strange at the rehearsals, but I figured he'd come around as soon as he got to know everybody. I had no idea he was going to leave and lay there wondering what would happen next. I had to call Elektra with the news and I wasn't sure whether they would still be as committed to the whole deal without Lonnie. The more I thought about it the less I cared and by the time the sun came up I had made up my mind that no matter what happened, I wasn't going to worry about it. The first thing I was going to do was to go back to Memphis and hire a road manager. If this tour was going to happen that was fine; if it didn't, that was fine too.

I called Elektra and told them what had happened. They asked if there was anyone I could think of to take Lonnie's place. "Of course. Furry Lewis," I said, without even knowing I was going to say it. Although they had never heard of Furry, they agreed to let me take him on the tour, something I will always be grateful for.

Later that afternoon, Tarp came to my room. "Come look in Lonnie's room. I think I found the reason he left." I followed him to the room, where a Gideon bible lay open on the desk. There was a phrase underlined in the bible that read "Get thee out of Zion." Well that must have been it. Old Lonnie got a sign and we got Furry Lewis. Not a bad swap.

I flew to Memphis and picked up Furry and talked my friend Paul Jaffe into coming along as road manager. Although Furry didn't need to rehearse, I took him back with me anyway so he could get to know everyone before the tour. Furry didn't see well and I got adjoining rooms and left the door open between them in case he needed anything. I had forgotten that no matter what time he went to bed, Furry always woke between five and six in the morning. He then woke me and I called room service and ordered his breakfast, then went back to bed for a few hours before rehearsal. I would have stayed up all night with him if I had to. It meant more than anything to me to be on this tour with him. Although Jeannie and the rest of the band didn't know Furry, by the end of the tour they grew to love him just as much as I did.

Since Elektra had never before subsidized a tour like ours, they weren't taking any chances. They wanted us to play three dates in Southern Louisiana as a trial run. I guess they figured if we were a complete flop, not many people would know about it, saving them any embarrassment. The three gigs were to be played in Baton Rouge, New Orleans, and Lafayette—the same town where I had all the trouble ten years before with the Mar-Keys.

After our rehearsals in Muscle Shoals, we returned to Memphis for a few days before flying to New Orleans, where we boarded a tour bus for the two-hour drive to Baton Rouge. Our bus driver was a no-nonsense, by-the-book guy with a crew cut named Albert. As we boarded his bus, I think he was probably asking himself what he had done to deserve such an outrageous crew as us: hippies and niggers, the scum of the earth. As soon as the bus started moving, the first thing Tarp did was fire one up. He cracked the window so as not to offend anyone, especially Albert, but it didn't fly. Albert got on his microphone and in a very efficient tone informed the lot of us that under no circumstances were the windows to be opened at any time, and that the use of illegal drugs could lead to incarceration by the nearest law enforcement agency. This announcement seemed to throw a damper on the excitement that was building about playing at last in front of a live audience that night. It was like being on tour with your dad. We rode the rest of the way in virtual silence.

We arrived in Baton Rouge and checked into a motel out on the highway surrounded by farmland. Albert drove us over to the gig that night and parked the bus in front of the sprawling nightclub called Willy Purple's. After everything was set up, I came out to the bus, where Albert sat alone. I asked him if he would like to come in and hear the band. He told me he would stay with the bus and, since it was such a hot night, he would keep the air conditioner going.

I went back inside and introduced Furry to the packed house. We decided to bring Furry on first before the whole band came on. I had told Furry to go out and sing for as long as he wanted and, when he was ready to come off, to look at me and wave. That first night the more Furry sang, the more the crowd wanted, and you could tell he was having a good time. I was watching the people's reaction to Furry from back-stage when I noticed a shiny little crew-cut head in the very back of the place. Damn if it wasn't Albert, standing there in the sea of longhairs, grinning like an idiot.

After Furry, Jeannie and I came out with that great band and choir and, for two hours, shook the place to its foundations. Even we were surprised at the audience's reaction. We came off stage that first night feeling like we had conquered the world. All the rehearsals had finally paid off, and we knew the show would work without changing a thing.

We went back to our motel for some rest before the drive to Lafayette the next morning. As usual, I had an adjoining room to Furry's with the door open. We talked for a while before I went to bed. I was almost asleep when I heard someone knocking on Furry's door. His light was still on, so I got up and peeked through the door to see who was there. Furry opened the door and there stood Albert. I jumped back in bed before anyone saw me and lay there for an hour, listening to the muffled voic-es coming from the next room. I have no idea what was said that night between Albert and Furry; I only know that as we boarded the bus the next morning, Albert was a different person. He greeted everyone as if he had known them for years and, during the drive to Lafayette, Furry sat in the front seat and the two of them carried on like old friends.

When we arrived in Lafayette, I was amazed at how much the place had changed for the better over the past ten years. The audience that night made us feel right at home. Back at the motel after the show, Albert again showed up at Furry's door and, as I slept, they talked well into the night. During the long ride to New Orleans, we played guitars and sang and smoked dope with the windows open. Albert even invited Fred Prouty up to do his famous impersonations over the P.A. Yes sir, Albert was a changed man.

We got to New Orleans late that afternoon and checked into the Holiday Inn in the French Quarter. That night we played the Ware-house, and I think it was probably the best show we played on the whole tour. The best part came during an encore, when I looked around and there was Albert on stage with us, dancing his ass off and laughing like a madman. On the way back to the motel, Albert informed us that he couldn't take us to the airport the next day, since he had a prior commitment to take a busload of basketball fans to Houston. Wayne, Tippy, and Marlin got their guitars out and we all sang "We're So Sorry, Uncle Albert." By the time we arrived at the motel, there were tears in his eyes as we told him goodbye. Albert had a wife and six kids, but I believe that if we had asked him, he would have left it all and gone with us.

We flew to Memphis that afternoon and changed planes for San Francisco. After a stop in Dallas, we settled back for the three-and-a-half-hour flight. After dinner, Furry got up and roamed the aisles doing magic tricks for the other passengers. I think it must have been a throw-back to the days when he played medicine shows from the back of a wagon with Gus Cannon all around the South. Anyway, he made close to fifty bucks that night doing his magic. Yep, American Airlines was the smoooooovest airline in the world.

We played Northern California for a week doing a live performance on KSAN before doing our last show in that part of the country, an out-door gig at the Monterey Peninsula. We carried a beautiful old rocking chair and a very expensive Persian rug from Elektra's West Coast offices. After Furry did his thirty minutes, he sat on stage, rocking on the rug with a cup of Ten High whiskey. If at any time during the rest of the show he felt like saying anything, he stood up and the band stopped playing 'til Furry had spoken his mind. He seldom did this, but on the afternoon we played Monterey, Furry stood up in midsong and walked slowly to the mike while we stopped playing and waited to hear what he had to say. The sky had been overcast all morning, but I swear, the moment Furry got to the mike, the sun broke through, lighting up his smiling face. He lifted his cup to the heavens, then uttered these words: "A chicken ain't nothin' but a bird. Thank you." He then sat down. The audience was the typical Northern California hippie set with their soap bubbles, frisbees, and lots of drugs. They had stopped where they were as Furry walked to the mike. They had no idea what Furry was talking about, but they knew it was heavy. You could hear shouts of "Wow," "Far out," and a few people seemed to faint dead away. The sun then disap-peared, as if Furry and God had planned the whole thing.

The last two nights of the tour were to be recorded for a live album. The first night of recording was at the Santa Monica Civic Auditorium. About twenty minutes before showtime, Furry and I were sitting in a small dressing room talking when Wayne Perkins rushed in and asked Furry if he had an extra bottleneck. Wayne lost his and, since he'd played mostly slide guitar, he was frantic. Furry told him he didn't have a spare but that he would be glad to make him one if provided the right supplies. He needed an empty wine bottle, which, with our crew, was an easy find; a shoestring, which Furry produced thanks to the shoe on his wooden leg; and some coal oil. Since the chances of finding coal oil backstage at the Santa Monica Civic Auditorium were slim to none, somebody came up with a can of lighter fluid, which, against his better judgment, Furry agreed to use, informing all present that coal oil was the ideal fuel for making a bottleneck.

He squirted an ample amount of lighter fluid into a glass ashtray on the dressing table. He held the shoestring in the air in a straight line and let it spiral down and around into the fluid, letting it soak for about thirty seconds. By this time, the dressing room was crowded with curious onlookers, not only members of the band but stagehands, lighting people, and half of Wally Heider's recording staff. To hell with 7000 people out front waiting on the show to start, this was history. Furry held onto the tip of the shoestring and pulled it back into the air. He then held the wine bottle near the bottom and slowly wound the shoestring around the base of the neck in a neat coil. You could hear a pin drop in the small dressing room. The shoestring in place, Furry pulled his old Zippo from his coat pocket, flicked it once, and passed the flame slowly beneath the string, igniting it into a slow burn. It took about a minute for the lighter fluid to burn off before Furry tapped the neck of the wine bottle ever so slightly against the edge of the dressing table. The neck broke off as clean as a breeze and rolled down the table while twenty-five people exhaled. Damn, it was beautiful.

We finished up at the Pasadena Civic Auditorium. Almost every night of the tour had been sold out, and we were all tired but happy. Late the next afternoon, Furry and I flew home aboard an American Airlines 707 that was less than twenty-five percent full. Once in a while, when you boarded an airliner, the pilot greeted you at the door, as was the case on this flight. Furry and I waited for the flight in the bar; consequently, Furry's proclamation of American Airlines being the smoovest airline in the world startled the smiling flight crew a little more than usual. The pilot introduced himself and shook hands with Furry before we took our seats toward the back of the aircraft.

After dinner, I laid down in three empty seats across from where Furry sat alone. I was almost asleep when the pilot came back and sat down next to Furry. I couldn't hear what was being said, but I could tell that, just like Albert in Louisiana, the pilot was curious and wanted to know what Furry was about. The one thing Furry loved to do more than anything was talk, especially if he had had a few cocktails, which he had this particular evening. But the pilot might as well have been talking to the wall. I laid there and watched as the man tried to make idle chit chat with Furry, who sat staring straight ahead as if he were sitting there by himself. After a few minutes, the pilot gave up and walked back to the flight deck, a bewildered look on his face.

I got up and went across the aisle. "Why didn't you talk to that guy?" I asked, "Aren't you feeling okay?"

He looked at me with that matter-of-fact look on his face. "He's the pilot, ain't he?" he answered. "He ain't got no business back here talking to me. He ought to stay up there and drive the plane." I think American Airlines dropped a few points in Furry's smoovest airline in the world chart that night.

I had left the Rolls at the airport, and by the time I drove Furry home, it was almost midnight. I parked under the streetlight in front of his house on Mosby and was taking his bags out of the trunk when, out of the corner of my eye, I saw someone walk out of the darkness. He had on a black beret and army fatigues, as did the four or five guys who followed him and formed a semicircle around me. Damned if it wasn't the Blue Gum brigade. The leader asked me, "What are you doing around here?" and I knew I was in trouble, but before I could answer, Furry came flying past me, his walking stick catching the head Blue Gum over the left ear.

"Ain't none of you business what he's doing around here!" Furry yelled. "Now you get on 'way from here, and I mean it!" I had never seen Furry this riled, as he stood in the street between me and the thugs.

"Okay, okay, ol' dude!" the leader called over his shoulder as the guys disappeared into the darkness, leaving me and Furry standing there very much relieved. As I carried his suitcase into the house, I thanked him for saving my ass. "It wasn't nothing," Furry said. "Besides, you ain't paid me yet."

Years later, I went to hear Lonnie Mack at a local club in Memphis and we resumed our friendship, and remain good friends to this day. It turned out he was going through a tough time when he left us in Muscle Shoals and, although I would have liked for him to tour with us, I'm forever happy that Furry got to go. It was definitely one of the high points of my life.

THE CONCERT FOR BANGLADESH

After resting up for a week, I flew back to L.A. to do some PR work at Elektra's West Coast office. I arrived the day they got word that their number-one act was dead. Jim Morrison had been found in his Paris apartment dead of a drug overdose, and the mood around the place was

George Harrison and Don Nix in Santa
Catalina, California, 1970.
Photo: Patti Boyd Harrison.

140

not what you would call festive. I stayed at a friend's house in the hills
who had worked for the Beatles at Apple Studios in London. George
Harrison was in town and dropped by one night and she introduced us.
The next day his wife, Patti, called to invite us on a cruise to Catalina.
Early the next morning, they picked us up for the drive to Marina Del
Rey, where we boarded an old Navy vessel that had been converted to a
pleasure craft.

We spent the day anchored off Catalina water skiing and watching
the seaplanes take off and land in the harbor. At one point, a nuclear
submarine came into port, the crew standing at attention on deck. It was
most impressive, and a little scary, since none of us had ever seen a

submarine, nuclear or otherwise. By mid-afternoon I still hadn't gotten my sea legs and was relieved when George told the crew to take us back to the mainland. Back on solid ground, everyone admitted being a little seasick, though no one had said anything for fear of being thought of as a weenie. Speaking for myself, I was glad to be off that boat.

George had rented a house in Benedict Canyon and invited me over the next day. He had brought along his dad, Harry, and close friend, Klaus Voorman. George was in the states trying to put a show together to raise money for Bangladesh. I had heard of concerts for hospitals, diseases, and just plain greed, but never one to raise money for an entire country. He asked if I could put together a soul choir to back the various acts he had asked to perform. I told him I would be happy to, and the next day I flew back to Memphis. Putting the choir together was easy and, when George called two days later, I told him I had asked Marlin and Jeannie Green, Claudia Linnear, and Don Preston, and they had agreed to perform. He asked if I would like to be in the choir as well and I, of course, agreed. This was some exciting stuff. George had lined up a terrific concert with Eric Clapton, Leon Russell, Billy Preston, Bob Dylan, and Badfinger. Ringo was going to be there and I knew that George had asked Lennon and McCartney to perform as well.

I flew to New York with Marlin and Jeannie a week before the August 2 concert set to take place in Madison Square Garden. We were met at the airport by a representative of Apple Records, and were taken to the Park Central Hotel, where George had booked the 27th floor for the musicians, singers, girlfriends, wives, and lovers to stay. We were given a yellow button as an identification badge to wear at all times, without which we would be denied access to the floor. There were guards at the elevator doors and security was tight, since it was possible that all four Beatles might show up. Although this didn't happen, George, Ringo, and John were there. George and Patti had a suite where nightly parties took place and everyone left their doors open. It was like some mad frat house where you might run into anyone in the halls. When word of the concert got out, everyone who wasn't in the show wanted to be and they dropped by to schmooze ol' George. Steven Stills, Judy Collins, Mama Cass, Peter Frampton, and a dozen others offered their services, but George had made up his mind exactly how the whole thing would run.

Although it was released later that the entire show had been an impromptu performance, several rehearsals were held in a piano recital hall above the Baldwin Piano Showroom in Manhattan. The showroom

Ringo Starr at rehearsal for the Concert for
Bangaladesh, New York City, 1971.
Photo: Don Nix.

was directly behind the hotel and could be easily reached by taking the
hotel service elevator to the kitchen, crossing an alley, and going up a
flight of stairs. Those present at the rehearsals were George, Billy Preston, Ringo, Badfinger, Jim Keltner, Klaus Voorman, the Hollywood
Horns, and the soul choir. John Lennon was to perform two Chuck
Berry songs, but on the third day of rehearsal, he pulled up stakes and
flew to Paris without telling anyone. It seemed he wanted Yoko to be
added to the show's lineup and, when George refused, he took his ball
and went home.

The week before the concert everyone was having a big time, but
George had to sprout wings to stay above the bullshit. He served as
babysitter, guru, and diplomat. There was one thing he couldn't cover
and that was the presence of Allen Klein and his toad, Pete Bennett.
Klein was handling some of the Beatles' and Stones' affairs until they
later found him out. He was a real low rent who preyed on people like
George Harrison. Pete Bennett was his yes-man and tried to dress and
act like a mafia don, which only made him look foolish. They served no
purpose at the rehearsals or the concerts but to intimidate and piss
people off.

On the night before the concert, a rehearsal was held in the empty
Madison Square Garden. We ran through the show a couple of times in
front of thousands of empty seats. It was downright eerie. Right before
rehearsals ended, his highness, Mr. Bobby Joe Dylan, appeared, but first
made Pete Bennett collect everybody's camera so no photographs could

be taken. Although he didn't have his sword cane with him, I figured if anybody tried to snap him, he'd probably pull a gun and shoot them dead where they stood.

The first show was to be at two in the afternoon, with the second to follow that evening at seven. For the most part, we had a good time and so did the audience. The only drawback came when the union refused to let the Apple film crew anywhere near the place. They insisted any filming had to be done by the Madison Square Garden crew, which turned out to be a catastrophe. Anyone who saw the movie can see how inept they were.

After the evening show, we were told to go to our rooms for an hour, then turn all the lights out, as if everyone on the 27th floor had gone to bed. It seemed that fans had rented rooms on the 27th floor of nearby hotels and were watching with binoculars in hopes of spotting their favorite Beatle with his drawers down. After everyone's lights were turned off, we met in the hallway, where again we took the service elevator to the kitchen, went out the back door, and went down the alley to the waiting limos. After making sure that no one was following, the limos dropped us at a small jazz club in the Village where an all-night party gave everyone a chance to relax and unwind. George went around and thanked everyone personally and made us all feel like we had done something special. Two days later, I flew back to Memphis accompanied by George's father, Harry, and Klaus Voorman. For the next two weeks we ate soul cooking and sat on Furry's floor listening to the blues.

In September of '71 I bought my first house, a beautiful old home near Overton Park in a well-to-do neighborhood of older, well-heeled Republicans. The grounds were beautifully landscaped with a Japanese garden, a greenhouse, and a small guesthouse. It was a comfortable place with fireplaces upstairs and down, and it even had an elevator near the back door that went to the master bedroom. There was a lot of room, especially for someone who had occupied a one-room flat for the past seven years, a flat I still paid rent on in case things didn't work out.

Two weeks after I moved into my new digs I flew to London, which shows just how excited I was about the new home. I hooked up with Isaac Tigrett, a Tennessee boy who had moved to England and opened an American burger restaurant called the Hard Rock Cafe at 151 Old Park Lane in the heart of London. He gave me a place to stay and sold me another Rolls Royce, which I shipped back to the states. I came home for Christmas, then returned to England and France, where I represented Stax at the annual Midem Convention in Cannes. It was there that I learned Packey Axton had died, a victim of his own self-destruction. The booze he had loved so much had eaten his stomach away until it killed him in February 1972.

Back in England at Isaac's house, I got together one afternoon with Jeff Beck, whom I had last seen in Memphis. He had been there the year before recording an album at Steve Cropper's new studio and had recorded one of my songs, "Going Down." Steve threw a party for Jeff and his band when the album was completed, at which time Jeff asked if I might be interested in producing his next album. Since everyone had had a lot to drink that night I didn't take him very seriously, but when he brought it up again that afternoon at Isaac's I told him I was definitely interested.

There was a lot happening in London in '72 and I stayed until spring before returning to Memphis. The Alabama State Troupers album was released and was selling well, but it wasn't the windfall Elektra had wanted. I knew my days there were numbered, but I didn't care. I had already made up my mind that I was a lot happier recording other artists than recording myself. Besides, to have a successful career as an artist I knew I would have to stay on the road a lot, something that didn't appeal to me at all.

Since there was not a lot happening recording-wise at Stax, I spent a lot of time in Muscle Shoals producing another Albert King album and recording songs I had written in England. The Muscle Shoals rhythm section had become so well-known that artists from all over the world were coming there to record. The English group Traffic not only came to record, but took the rhythm section on tour to augment their band. It was after this tour that Traffic's record label owner, Chris Blackwell, signed the rhythm section as artists. Although they could have produced themselves or had their pick of anyone they had worked with, they asked me to produce the album. It was not only a great honor but another chance to work with the best recording band I have ever heard.

The basic players were still the same: Roger Hawkins played drums, Barry Beckett keyboards, David Hood bass, and Jimmy Johnson rhythm guitar. There were other guitarists who could be called on depending on what a certain producer wanted. Eddie Hinton, Pete Carr, and Wayne Perkins each added their distinctive sound to the album. Since instrumentals weren't selling well in '72, we decided to ask some local singers to participate in the sessions. Carrol Quillen, Eddie Hinton, George Soule, Steve Winwood, and Smith, Perkins, and Smith performed songs

144

Don Nix, Klaus Voorman, and George Harrison
at Henley on Thames, 1974.

Mercedes McCambridge, Eddie Hinton, and Don Nix
in Muscle Shoals Sound Studio, 1969.

DRIVING SOLO

for the album; Winwood sang and played organ on two cuts. It was one of the best times I had in Muscle Shoals, and the album turned out better than expected. It seemed to be representative of the music coming from that area at that particular time and I was proud of it. But in the end it was not to be. Before the album could come out, there was a falling out between Chris Blackwell and Jimmy Johnson, and it was never released.

BECK, BOGERT, AND APATHY

In the fall of '72 I finally heard from Jeff Beck. He had teamed up with Carmine Appice and Tim Bogert, two New Yorkers who had played with Vanilla Fudge and Cactus. The three had tried producing themselves and had cut a few tracks at Chess Studios in Chicago before calling me to finish the album. We all met at O'Hare Airport one cold afternoon in November, at which time I discovered that the only person with a credit card was me. Do you already have the feeling this is not going to turn out well? There were a lot of promises about paying me back as soon as the album was finished and I didn't seem to have a choice. If I'd only excused myself, gone in to the restroom, and thought for fifteen seconds about turning over a major credit card to a teacake and two Yankees from Long Island, who voluntarily named their first band Vanilla Fudge, I probably would have got a first-class ticket on the first thing smoking back to Memphis, but I didn't.

147

The credit card was immediately put to use to rent a car and as soon as we pulled out of the airport, Tim Bogert unscrewed the door lock covers and threw them out the window, while Carmine put his boot heel through the overhead light, crushing it to bits. When I asked the reasoning behind these acts of vandalism they told me, "We always trash our rental cars." These guys were not using live ammo.

The next day, we went to Chess Studios, where two years before I had had so much fun recording with Leon, Freddy, Duck, and the Shelter people. This time was a completely different story. The studio had officially closed down, but had remained open at Jeff Beck's request because his lifelong dream had been to record there. The only problem was that half the recording equipment had been dismantled, including the playback monitors. The situation did not lend itself to recording memorable music, but the band, who had decided to call themselves Beck, Bogert, and Appice, insisted we try. Of course, it didn't work out, and after three days of futile attempts at recording anything decent, we decided to go elsewhere. I took a last look around the old studio before I left and I thought of all the great musicians who had played, sang, drank, fought, and laughed inside these walls while recording some of the best music the world would ever know. That night we flew to Los Angeles.

Jeff's manager had booked time at Village Recorders, which was a decent studio. But I learned right away that it wasn't so much the studio as the musicians at fault for the terrible sound we were putting on tape. The main trouble lay in the fact that Bogert and Appice had no concept of a groove. They were from some weird school of thinking that the more you played, the better it sounded. It sounded like a drummer and a bass player taking four-minute solos while Beck picked his way through the corpses. Appice had every drum known to man set up in the studio with double bass drums, quadruple tom-toms, and cymbals forever. He even had a huge gong set up behind him which, thank God, he never hit. At one point in the recording he told me I should have more mikes on his drums, which I agreed to. For looks the engineer went out and set up several mikes, which were never patched in and although we never told him, Carmine thought it sounded much better.

Jeff and I ate together in the evenings, and one night I asked him why he had teamed up with such lightweights. He told me it was a management decision and, although he didn't particularly like it, he was going to play it out. I liked Jeff, but he seemed like a sad person who rarely laughed. He was depressed most of the time except for when he played, and then he came alive, almost like a different person. One night, we went to the Roxy and got loaded. He told me he had always wanted to sing, but had never dared record his voice. We had recorded a track of a song I wrote called "Black Cat Moan," which had no vocal on it, so we went by the studio that night and I talked him into singing it. It took three hours, but it was the most fun I had on the whole project.

I went back to Memphis just before Christmas and did the remix at Ardent with John Fry, but no matter how hard we tried, there was not enough on tape to make a decent single, much less an album.

After New Year's '73, I took the finished album to New York and played it for the band and their managers. They, of course, thought it sounded great. I had already made plans to fly to London from New York and, as chance had it, so were Carmine and Bogert. Their manager took us to the airport the next evening, where we boarded a British Airways flight.

I came on after everyone had been seated and, of course, the only vacant seat was right between the Long Island rock stars. Carmine had stashed his stick bag and various other carry-on items under the seat in front of me, which made it impossible to sit comfortably on the long flight. At the ticket counter, the flight was billed as a 747, which I loved, but at the gate the agent had informed me that since there weren't enough people to half fill the larger aircraft, we were being put aboard a smaller Viscount, which is about the size of a DC-9. I sat there for a few minutes, getting mad as well as claustrophobic. I jumped up and without saying a word to anyone, I walked to the front of the plane where the agent was closing the door.

"Excuse me!" I said. "I'm getting off," as I squeezed through the half-closed door. The guy looked at me like I had slapped him.

"But you can't get off," he said, opening the door all the way. "If you'll take a close look, you'll see that I am off and I ain't gettin' back on," I told him.

About that time the head stewardess walked up and asked what was going on. "He's getting off," the agent told her. She aimed her stern hands-on-hip stare at me. "You can't get off," she said in an aggravated tone. This was getting good. Before I could reply, the door to the flight deck opened, and the captain stuck his head through the door and asked what the holdup was.

"This man is getting off," the agent told him, which brought the captain's whole body out real fast.

"Why are you getting off?" the captain asked in his clipped British accent.

"I don't like this airplane," I told him, "and I don't feel safe on it."

He then asked if I had checked a bag on the flight and I told him I had, but assured him there was no bomb in it. He tried once more to coax me back aboard, but I stood firm.

"If you can change your mind about what kind of airplane I'm gonna fly on, then I ought to be able to change my mind about flying on it," which seemed to make sense to the captain. He told the agent to give me my ticket back and he would leave my luggage at Heathrow. By the time I got out of the airport, it was almost midnight and I felt great. I took a cab to Manhattan and spent the night with an old girlfriend. The next morning, I took a cab back to JFK, where I boarded an eleven o'clock flight on a half-full 747 and slept like a baby all the way to London.

I wasn't surprised that it took eight months to be reimbursed for the $5,000 the band had charged to my credit card.

✳   ✳   ✳

I was still staying at Isaac Tigrett's flat in Kensington, except for the occasional trips I made to Henley-on-Thames to visit George and Klaus. I had written a couple of songs during one of these visits, and George asked if I would like to use Apple Studios to record them. Klaus offered to play bass and I rounded up some Alabama boys who were in London promoting their new album, *Smith, Perkins and Smith,* for Island Records. Wayne Perkins and Tim and Steve Smith filled out the band, and a week later I recorded two tracks that, along with the sessions I had cut in Alabama the summer before, were enough to complete an album.

The day after the recording, Wayne Jackson called from Memphis to tell me Charlie Freeman had died of a drug overdose in Austin, Texas.

When I came back to Memphis a few months later, I played the new songs for Jim Stewart at Stax. Jim was excited about the tracks and, since he was one of the few people I trusted in the music business, I agreed to a one-album contract. The album, *Hobos and Heroes,* was released three months later.

MAYALL MADNESS

Right before my Stax album came out, I got a call from John Mayall, who asked if I was interested in producing his tenth anniversary album for Polydor. I had never met John, although I was familiar with his music, and I accepted his offer. Two days later, I was in L.A. at his house in Laurel Canyon and did not leave for three months. It was to be a summer to beat all summers. I had never met anyone like John. He was a true Renaissance man. He had built his house himself, a sprawling multilevel job on the top of a hill that from the rear overlooked the canyon and from the front gave a breathtaking view of Hollywood and L.A.

John was an artist who photographed and designed most of his album covers. He was a stonemason, a carpenter, and in a small sewing room he made most of his clothes. John was born in Manchester, England, and as a teenager lived in a treehouse he had built. He was one of the few people from his home town to serve in the Korean War. He was a songwriter and poet, and his Shepherd's pie was so good I've seen people almost come to blows over the last helping. His house was like an amusement park. There was a full bar upstairs and, on the lower level, a swimming pool with a steam room and a small cinema where you could take your pick of hundreds of movies. On any given day that summer, there were several young ladies sunbathing by the pool, most of whom were sans swimwear. I never wanted to leave.

We did the album at Sunset Sound Studios and had it finished in two weeks. We had a good time during the recordings, especially since he had put together such a diverse crew. There was Red Holloway on sax, Blue Mitchell on trumpet, Freddie Robinson playing guitar, Victor Gaskin on bass, Keef Hartley on drums, and Sugar Cane Harris on fiddle. After we finished the album, I took the tapes back to Memphis to do the remix with John Fry at Ardent. I then met Mayall in New York, where I mastered the album before we played it for the higher-ups at Polydor. They seemed pleased and we rushed back to L.A. for some more fun at John's house—a lot more fun. The well-stocked bar almost turned out to be our downfall. We drank Heineken and vodka all day and night, which leaves my memory of that summer a little fuzzy. Most of the fun was harmless and consisted of chatting up the endless stream of beautiful women and playing strange pranks on people.

One of these practical jokes backfired on John's birthday. His 75-year-old mom, Beryl, flew in from England to help celebrate. She was a frail, sweet lady who spoke with a proper English accent while chain-smoking Virginia Slims, and could outdrink any two people without falling down. The birthday party was to be held at Mon Maison restaurant and would be attended by about twelve people, including his manager, accountant, and a couple of lawyers who handled John's affairs. The afternoon before the party and after several drinks, John and I decided to go in disguise and drove down to Melrose, where we shopped for the right attire. At a cheap wig shop, John picked out a businessman's salt-and-pepper toupee with matching mustache, while I went for a large afro number that made me look slightly top-heavy. After a visit to a used clothing store we were set, and went home to get ready for the party.

John had called his manager and asked him to come by and pick up his mom since he had to make a few stops on the way to the restaurant. After attaching the mustache and filling his cheeks with tissue, John somehow got his long hair under the salt-and-pepper wig and dressed himself in an outfit not unlike a leisure suit. I dressed in semi-Superfly attire and pulled the afro over my head. Together we looked like a pimp and a tractor salesman, which was not exactly the look we had planned on, but by this time, we were so drunk it really didn't matter.

We arrived at the restaurant and, after telling the maître d' about our prank, we were seated at a table next to the birthday party. As we sat down, a few of the revelers glanced over at us, but paid little attention.

John Mayall, Mike Gardener, and Don Nix,
High Cotton Bar, Memphis, 1974.

We thought, "Great, it's working," but the longer we sat there the dumber we felt. At one point, John leaned over about two feet from his mom's face and asked in a terrible French accent whose birthday was being celebrated. He was basically told to get stuffed. We drank several glasses of wine, but by this time the heat was starting to take its toll. Sweat was pouring down our necks from the unventilated hairpieces, and the tissue in John's cheeks had started to gum up. We sat there like a couple of fools not having planned any farther than this. We finally gave in and, although everyone was surprised, it was anticlimactic since by this time we were too sick to think about eating birthday cake. John and I became like brothers and remain close friends to this day. I spent a lot of time at his house in years to come, where every day was a holiday.

Under heavy protest, I went back on tour the first part of November using Larry Raspberry and his band, the Highsteppers, as backing group. I took Tarp Tarrant along as a second drummer as well as a three-girl singing group that included Larry's beautiful wife, Carol. The Raspberrys had been close friends of mine for years, and I had sat in with them at different clubs around town so many times, I felt like part of their band. Larry's first band, the Gentrys, had scored big in 1965 with a hit called "Keep on Dancing" and he is still the best rock-'n'-roll act I've ever seen. The Highsteppers consisted of Greg "Fingers" Taylor on harmonica, Wild Bill Marshall on drums, Rocky Berretta on bass, and the great Jay Spell on keyboards.

My Stax album was doing surprisingly well, and Jim Stewart asked if I could go on the road to help promote it. We traveled for the next six months playing mini-tours in different parts of the country, then returning home to play club gigs at the High Cotton and Lafayette's Music Room. By this time, I had really started to slip and my drinking was out of control. The booze, mixed with the Valium and other assorted chemicals, was causing my behavior to become erratic and sometimes even psychotic. I had always taken pride in the fact that I could maintain a pretty even keel no matter what or how much I had consumed, but that became the exception and not the rule. Not only did it cost me friends, but it brought my self-esteem to an all-time low and I started to withdraw. As I look back, I at least had the good sense to stay away from people if I couldn't behave myself.

In the fall of 1973, I sold my house in Midtown and bought a larger one in the posh neighborhood of Chickasaw Gardens. I really didn't

Don Nix, Larry Raspberry, and the Highsteppers
at Lafayette's Music Room, Memphis, 1975.

care about having a big house or a Rolls Royce, but it seemed at the time like the right thing to do. For the first time in my life I had more money than I could spend, and I found out the hard way that money can lead to boredom. I mean, if you've got the money to buy anything you want, then the things you buy are not that important.

I bought the house from a nice old couple in their nineties who were moving to a retirement home. On the way to their attorney's office for the closing, I took a couple of quaaludes and, while all the legal papers were being read and signed, I dozed off. Evidently, it took quite a while to wake me and, if it hadn't been for the briefcase full of money that I had brought along, I think they would have called the whole thing off. After the deal went through I got into my big white Rolls and, as I backed out of my parking space, I smashed into the front of the old people's

ROAD STORIES AND RECIPES

car. I got out to see what damage I had done and fell flat on my face. I don't know how long I lay there, but when I did get up, the old people were gone, glad to be rid of me I know.

The last leg of the tour was to start in the spring of '74 and would cover every major city on the West Coast, where we were joined by Claudia Linnear. I got sloshed every night and, in San Francisco, during a live broadcast from the stage of the Great American Music Hall, things got so crazy that KSAN had to return to their normal programming. John Mayall had flown up to sit in and the two of us proved too much for the airwaves.

My health was getting worse, and I had to be taken to the emergency room in Portland and again the next night in Seattle. I had not been eating and was suffering from the flu and strep throat. By the time the tour was over, I was a complete wreck. John took me back to his house in Laurel Canyon to recuperate and I again stayed for most of the summer. When I got back to Memphis, Jim Stewart asked me to go to London to produce Skin Alley, an English group he had just signed to Stax. Although I was only there for three weeks, I managed to come home with not only the finished album but another Rolls, which I needed like a heart attack.

KILLING GROUND

One evening Duck Dunn, Larry and Carol Raspberry, and a few others dropped by my house for a small party. We were sitting around on the floor drinking wine when about midnight, Eric Clapton walked in with his wife, Patti. He had played Memphis that evening and the two of them were roaring pretty good. Everyone but Duck left and the four of us ended up in my bedroom sitting on the floor. We were all in pretty rough shape so when Eric spotted my 9 mm pistol lying under the bed, I offered to let him shoot it. He told me he had never shot a gun, and damn right he wanted to shoot it. At the time, it seemed like a great idea and I thought I was being a wonderful host.

We went downstairs and into the rear of the house which, in our condition, took a while. I stood behind him as Eric pointed the pistol toward the ground, but his aim was not what you would call steady and the pistol was weaving all over the place. I took his hand and the two of us managed to keep the gun pointed away from his foot. It was 3 A.M. and not a sound could be heard when he pulled the trigger. My first thought was, "Damn, that's a lot louder than I thought it was going to be!" and I stepped back a few feet, but the sound didn't seem to bother Eric, and I think the muzzle flash kind of hypnotized him for a second. Anyway, it felt good to him, and he let go with seven more rounds and kept clicking the pistol long after it was empty. All that racket scared me and Duck, and we ran for his car, sure the cops would be there any second. We pushed Patti and Eric into the small back seat of the Pinto and went roaring down the long driveway. About the time we got to the street, it dawned on me that I was running away from my own house, but the shape I was in it didn't much matter.

Duck had moved to a house in the country where he and June kept horses. The Pinto was his farm car and the back was full of bridles, empty feed sacks, and other horse stuff. It smelled like a barn, but our passengers didn't seem to mind, especially Patti, who was starting to fade. We drove around for half an hour trying to find the river, where they were staying at the Holiday Inn Rivermont. We drove down Crump Boulevard and turned off a small side street and I asked Duck where he was going. He just looked at me with that "you don't mean to tell me I'm driving" stare.

It was not the best part of town to be lost in, especially at three-thirty in the morning. The county elections were coming up and there were political posters on every telephone pole. One of the candidates was named Opp Oppenheimer, and Patti remarked that such a poster would look good on her wall back in England. Duck slammed on the brakes and, being proper Southern gentlemen, we jumped out and ripped several of them down, which we shoved into the back seat.

Duck kept driving until we reached a construction site that blocked the small street; wooden sawhorses had been erected with blinking yellow caution lights. Once again, from the back seat, Patti told us how she had always wanted one of those. So, while Duck turned the car around, I jumped out and grabbed four of the battery-powered lights and placed them in the back, where things were starting to get a little crowded. We finally found our way back to a street we recognized, and made our way to Riverside Drive, where the hotel was located. Everyone had fallen silent for the rest of the trip, but every now and then I turned to look at Eric and Patti in the back seat, surrounded by their loot. Every time one of the emergency lights blinked, I caught a glimpse of the two of them, eyes glazed, staring straight ahead. Blink, Eric and Patti, Opp Oppenheimer, blink, Eric and Patti, Opp Oppenheimer, blink blink, Eric and Patti, Opp Oppenheimer.

157

ROAD STORIES AND RECIPES

I didn't work again until the winter of '75, when Keef Hartley called and asked if I would come to England to produce an English folk singer named Michael Chapman. I told him I couldn't wad a shotgun with what I knew about folk music. He told me Michael was a good friend of Mayall's and that I would really like working with him. Although I wasn't in any kind of shape, mentally or physically, to make the trip, I agreed to go. Two weeks later I was again on the 7 P.M. Pan Am flight from New York to London, armed with a pocket full of quaaludes and a half gallon of Remy Martin.

By the time Keef picked me up at Heathrow the next morning, I was a raving lunatic. He took me to meet Max Hole, who was Michael's manager and the man who was paying the bills. I was still sipping on the cognac, but I was down to my last two quaaludes, which I decided to save for an emergency. I think I kind of scared Max, and I'm sure he thought he had made a mistake in his choice of producers. After lunch, I asked him when I was going to meet Michael. It seemed like the subject had been avoided all day. Finally, Max told me that Michael didn't exactly live in London, and that I would fly to Newcastle that evening and Michael would pick me up and drive me to his house near Greenhead, Scotland. I was to stay there for a week getting to know Michael and maybe writing a few songs for the album. We spent most of the afternoon in a pub and by the time I got to the airport, I could barely stand. I had an hour's wait before the flight and used the time to try and straighten myself up. I did not want my first meeting with Michael to end up with him carrying me off the plane.

As always, I was the last person to board and the only empty seat was next to a guy in an overcoat who was visibly shaken. As I sat down, I noticed he was wearing a white uniform beneath the coat. As the plane taxied for takeoff, he confided in me that he worked in a mental hospital on one of the Channel Islands and this was his first airplane flight. I asked him why he hadn't taken the train, and he told me his grandmother had just died and his family would be at the airport to pick him up. Just as the plane turned to take off, he reached into his coat pocket and pulled out a pint of Irish Whiskey and took a long pull before offering the bottle to me. I had never acquired a taste for whiskey, but accepted it to wash down one of my emergency quaaludes and, since one good turn deserves another, offered the last one to my new-found friend. The guy was so rattled, he took it without asking what it was.

By the time we landed in Newcastle, the whiskey was gone and so were we. Since both of us were having trouble with our balance, we waited until everyone had left the plane before we stumbled off. The airport was closed and the plane was parked on the tarmac, where our luggage was being lined up to claim. I had gotten so caught up in the guy's grief that, when he introduced me to his family as one of his best friends, they assumed I had accompanied him to Newcastle for the funeral. We were all in a circle hugging and crying when, out of the corner of my eye, I saw a figure standing behind us who had to be Michael. I waved him over, introduced him around, and, after he had hugged everyone and offered the proper condolences, he helped me to the car.

After an hour's drive, we arrived at the beautiful old farmhouse he shared with his wife, Andru. By the time I got to bed it was 2 A.M. and I had been up for almost 48 hours. I fell fast asleep and when I woke the sun was up. I went downstairs and asked what time it was. Andru told me it was ten o'clock and, when I expressed surprise at not having slept longer, she told me it was ten o'clock Tuesday morning and I had been asleep for thirty-one hours. The rest did me good and, for the remainder of the week, my days were spent sleeping and sightseeing and the nights were spent at the local pub. I had never passed out from consuming too much of anything, and the next day could remember almost everything that happened, which in some cases was not too big a blessing. The same couldn't be said for Michael. One night, after bringing me home, he went out again and woke me the next morning to ask if I had heard anything during the night. I told him I had slept sound and asked what had happened. He told me to come downstairs for a look. We went outside and there was his car lying on its right side, its wheels sticking out like some large dead animal; Michael had no idea how it got that way. With the help of some local miners, the car was righted, but the mystery was never solved.

The next day we packed for the long drive to Fowey, South Cornwall, where the tracks were to be recorded at Sawmill Studio. Fowey was the last village before Land's End at the tip of England and was located on the Fowey River. We arrived about 10 P.M., and a light rain began to fall. The studio had been an old barrel mill and could only be reached by river. There were two people with a small boat whom the studio had sent to get us, but Keef and the other musicians were nowhere to be found.

It was pitch black and only a few lights could be seen in the village. As we stood by the dock, a sound like a chorus of angels came floating down the darkness and out over the water. We followed the sound up the small stone street and into a pub in the middle of town. The closer we got, the more beautiful the singing became, until we opened the door and found almost everyone from the village in the middle of their weekly Sunday night sing-along. It was amazing. As soon as one song ended, someone started another and everybody joined in. The harmonies were perfect and you could tell that this had been going on for generations.

Keef had a table with the other musicians where Michael, Andru, and I ordered a pint and joined in the singing. I only wish I had known all the songs, for there were no inhibitions in this place. Everyone sang every song full-tilt, holding nothing back. We stayed until the last song was sung before taking the boat to the studio. Sitting in that boat in the darkness with the mist falling, I couldn't get over what I had just heard. It was definitely a spiritual experience, and I hoped we could drag the sessions out long enough to be there for the next Sunday night sing-along.

Besides Keef on drums, there was Rick Kemp on bass, Peter Wood on keyboards, and Tim Renwick and Andy Latimer on guitars. They were good players and we had the tracks finished by Friday, then drove to London to do the overdubs. One morning I walked into the studio and someone handed me a newspaper. On the front page I read that Stax Records had closed its doors and ceased to exist. After three weeks in London, I flew home and, although I had a good time working with Michael and the band, my heart wasn't in it anymore and I knew this would be my last trip for a long while.

When I got home I discovered my house had been broken into and most of my rich-man stuff had been hauled off. A neighbor, whom I didn't know, told me a few days later that he had seen several men loading my possessions into a van. He assumed that I had sold the house and was moving. I was moving alright, only somebody forgot to tell me where.

The guys who robbed me actually did me a favor, for it taught me no matter how much money you have or how much stuff you buy, there's always going to be somebody trying to take it away from you. It might be burglars, the bank, the IRS, or the Grim Reaper. In the end, nobody keeps any of it. I made up my mind to sell the house, the cars, and anything else that was left as soon as possible. Being a man of means just wasn't my M.O. and I couldn't wait to get back to life in the cheap seats.

160

EPILOGUE

The rain was falling harder and the wind blew it under the entrance way where I had fallen asleep. I scooted back into the darkness and realized that this was the first time I had been back to my old school since I started here twenty years ago. In some ways, the time had flown by and, in others, it seemed like an eternity. I had not kept in touch with any of my class-mates except the guys in the Mar-Keys. I missed them. Guys like Joe Clayton, Douglas Massey, and Delbert Coggins. Where were they and what were they doing? I missed this old school and the safe haven it provided while I was a student.

It's funny how important people and places are long after they're gone. I missed Charlie and Packey and Dewey. I missed Duke's, the Casi-no, the Sky-Vue Drive-In, the PI, and Stax. The cotton carnival was gone and Main Street was being bricked over and converted to a mall. All of these were just memories now of people and places that had been so important to me growing up in Memphis. As I write this, it sounds like I was feeling sorry for myself, and that might be a small part of it. But mostly, for the first time in my life I felt lost and unconnected. It was like living under water and I had no idea how to make it any better.

The sun was coming up behind the gray sky and, in an hour or so, the first students would be arriving for class. I got up and walked slowly down the steps to the Rolls. I drove home, took three quaaludes, and slept for ten years.

UPDATE

On June 1, 1985, I got up and flushed everything down the toilet: the grass, pills, cigarettes, and eight bottles of imported beer. It was either that or die. I stayed high all night and slept all day and I was sick of it. It was eleven days before I slept again, the Valium withdrawals punishing me for all the years of abuse. I knew that the punishment would go on for months. Just when I thought I couldn't take it anymore, God sent me some help.

In the first week of September, I met Katrina Robbins, who had come up from Muscle Shoals to attend the Memphis art academy. We fell in love and, although she was twenty-five years younger than I, and everybody tried to stop it, we were married six months later. She not only saved me, she gave me a reason to live and get back the self-esteem that had been missing for so long. I don't want to sound too hokey here, but no matter how much I write, I could never express how good the last ten years have been with her. In 1987 we had a son, Jackson, and two years later we had Sam. In 1990, we moved to the rolling hills of middle Tennessee, just south of Nashville, where I've started writing again. We live near the woods in a comfortable home. We have a dog, a cat, six goldfish, two lovebirds, two finches, and three hermit crabs. We have a van, a fireplace, and a wild night at our house is a knock-down, drag-out pillow fight. Maybe not a Norman Rockwell painting, but a normal, happy life. A life I never thought I would have during my vacant years.

Sam, Don, Katrina, and Jackson Nix, 1996.
Photo: Jim Chappell.

DRIVING SOLO

RECIPES

Carrot and Orange Soup

INGREDIENTS:
Carrots
Orange rind
Onions
Potatoes
Milk
Salt and pepper
Sprig of parsley

Sauté onions and sweat the potatoes and carrots. Put the whole lot in the blender. Add water, orange rind, and one cup of milk. Put back in large pan and simmer for 20 minutes. Add salt and pepper. Serve with sprig of parsley.

This soup incredibly changes your whole attitude to life and, once rubbed well and truly all over your body, it gives you a magnetic attraction with female rodents! Mmmmm!

Dave Stewart

Easy and Italian!

INGREDIENTS:
Mozzarella cheese
Tomatoes
Basil (fresh)
Olive oil
Salt and pepper

Instructions: None (that's why it's easy). You just need the best ingredients-a sharp knife and a plate-and a good sense of slicing judgment. I could live on this for at least a week.

Annie Lennox

Carol Raspberry's Seafood over Wild Rice

INGREDIENTS:
1 pound shrimp
1/2 pound scallops
1 pound fresh mushrooms
1/2 pound crabmeat
3 Tb onions
4 Tb butter
1 1/2 cups of half & half and milk combined
Garlic powder to taste or fresh garlic minced
1/4 cup flour
1/2 tsp dry mustard and salt to taste
3 Tb dry sherry
1 cup Swiss or Gruyère cheese

Sauté together shrimp, scallops, crabmeat, mushrooms, and garlic powder in butter until just underdone. Sauté separately onions and butter. Mix half & half and milk, flour, mustard, and salt in blender and add to onions over medium heat. Add dry sherry now. Stir constantly. While thickening, add the 1 cup of cheese until melted. Add shrimp, scallops, mushrooms, and crabmeat until mixed. Serve over wild rice. Serves 8-10.

Carol Raspberry

165

ROAD STORIES AND RECIPES

Larry Raspberry's Artichoke Dip

INGREDIENTS:
2 cans artichokes (water packed, large), chopped
    very fine
1 1/2 cups parmesan cheese
1 1/2 cups mayonnaise
Chopped chives
Pepper to taste

Mix all ingredients together in a casserole dish and
bake in the oven at 350° for 30-45 minutes or until
golden brown.

This is a very easy recipe and serves about 8.
Makes a great appetizer. I have never served
this anywhere that people did not ask for the
recipe. Enjoy!

Larry Raspberry

Green Chili Pork Stew

INGREDIENTS:
2 lb pork cut into 1/2" cubes
2 Tb peanut oil
1 can (29 oz) white hominy, drained
1 can (7 oz) diced green chilies
2 cans (12 oz each) tomatillos, drained and crushed
2 yellow onions, diced
4 cloves garlic, minced
1 rib celery, diced
1 Tb cilantro, minced
1 tsp salt or to taste
1/2 tsp each of white pepper and oregano
Chicken stock to cover (1 qt or more)

Brown pork in oil. Remove and add onion, celery, and garlic. Cook until wilted. Return pork and add all other ingredients. Cover with chicken stock. Bring to a boil. Then lower heat and simmer 3 hours or until meat is tender.

Homemade chicken stock is preferred. If in a hurry, use 5 or 6 cans of chicken broth. If using fresh tomatillos, peel outer skin and put 1 dozen in a blender, chop, and add 1 tsp vinegar. Any fresh hot peppers should be roasted, seeded, and peeled. Trim all excess fat from pork. Serve in bowls. This meal will set you free and erase your blues!

Tim Drummond

Texas Chicken Fried Steak
(with gravy)

INGREDIENTS:
Tenderized round steak
Vegetable oil
Flour
Salt and pepper
Egg, beaten
Milk
Mashed potatoes
Biscuits

Pour oil about 1/3" deep in large frying pan and heat to frying temperature. Salt and pepper steak, cover with flour, then dip in beaten egg. Cover with flour again. Lay steak in frying pan and brown on both sides (golden brown). Then cover pan and cook another 5 to 7 minutes or until steak is done throughout. (Remember to leave steak plenty of room in the pan.) Remove steak from grease onto paper towels and pour some grease out of the pan, leaving all steak crumbs in the pan along with just enough grease to barely cover the bottom. Reduce fire to very low and add salt and plenty of black pepper to grease. Scrape with spatula so as not to burn. Slowly, add a little milk at a time, constantly stirring and scraping with spatula. Cook to desired consistency. Serve with mashed potatoes and biscuits.

Lee Roy Parnell

Denise LaSalle's Southern Pancakes

INGREDIENTS:

1 cup sifted self-rising flour

1 Tb cornmeal

1/4 tsp baking powder

1 egg

3 Tb oil

1/2 cup buttermilk

Mix first five ingredients, then add buttermilk until batter is to your satisfaction. Makes about six medium pancakes.

Denise LaSalle

Hot 'n' Spicy Chunky Beef Chili

INGREDIENTS:
2 1/4 lb lean boneless beef chuck, cut into
    3/4" pieces
1 cup coarsely chopped onion
2 cloves garlic, minced
2 Tb vegetable oil
1 tsp salt
1 can (28 oz) plum tomatoes, broken up
1 cup water
1 can (6 oz) tomato paste
3 Tb chili powder
1 tsp dried oregano leaves
1/2 tsp crushed red pepper pods
1 cup chopped green bell pepper
6 Tb each shredded cheddar cheese and sliced
    green onions

Brown beef (half at a time) with onion and garlic in
oil in large frying pan or dutch oven. Pour off drippings. Sprinkle salt over beef. Add tomatoes, water,
tomato paste, chili powder, oregano, and crushed red
pepper. Cover tightly and simmer 1 1/2 hours or until
beef is tender. Add green pepper and continue cooking
uncovered, 30 minutes. Sprinkle each serving with
cheese and green onion slices. 8 servings of 1 1/2
cups each. 333 calories, 36g protein, 16g fat, 13g
carbohydrate, 5.7 mg iron, 731 mg sodium, and
102 mg cholesterol. Enjoy!!!

Reba McEntire

Sautéed Chicken and Kielbasa

INGREDIENTS:
3 chicken breasts, cut into bite-sized pieces
1 polska kielbasa, cut into bite-sized pieces
1 bell pepper, cut in strips
1 large onion, cut in strips
2 cloves garlic
1 large tomato, diced
1 cup dry white wine
White rice

Sauté chicken in large skillet with a little vegetable oil. Remove chicken and set aside. Sauté pepper and onions slightly and add kielbasa and garlic
(crushed) until peppers and onions are soft. Pile
chicken on top of kielbasa mixture and diced tomato
on top of chicken. Add white wine, cover, reduce
heat, and simmer for 30 minutes. Serve over rice.

Butch Trucks

Louise's Lemon Dessert

INGREDIENTS:

3 egg yolks
1/8 teaspoon salt
1/2 cup sugar
1/4 cup fresh lemon juice
1/2 tsp grated lemon rind
3 egg whites
1 cup whipped cream or Cool Whip
1 cup crushed vanilla wafers

Beat egg yolks, salt, and sugar in top of double
boiler. Stir in lemon juice and grated rind. Cook
over hot (not boiling) water until mixture thickens
and coats spoon. Remove from heat and chill. Beat egg
whites until stiff. Fold in whipped cream and cooked
mixture until well-mixed. Sprinkle half of crushed
wafer crumbs evenly in bottom of baking dish or
freezer tray. Pour in lemon mixture (should be about
3/8" to 1/2" deep). Top with remaining wafer crumbs.
Freeze until firm. Serve in 3" squares.

This is easier to make than it sounds and you
won't believe how great it tastes!

David Hood

172

Lonnie Mack's Mexican Delight

INGREDIENTS:

1 small onion, diced
1 lb Velveeta cheese
4 oz mild cheddar
1 oz Monterey Jack
1 oz mozzarella
2 small jalapeños, diced
4 oz picante sauce (hot Pace preferred)
Milk
Tortilla chips

Brown onion with small amount of water over medium heat. Leave onions in and reduce heat to low. Add 3 Tb milk and thinly sliced cheeses, stirring constantly. When blended, add jalapeños and picante sauce. Add milk to desired thickness. Serve hot with tortilla chips. Serve as a sauce on refried beans, tacos, enchiladas, chili, or hamburgers.

Lonnie Mack

173

Texas Chili

A Brief History: The word *chili* (pronounced "chee-lee") is an Aztec word, but the Spanish version commonly used now is *chile* (pronounced "chee-lay"). Both words refer to the fruit of the *Capsicum annum* plant, which was, because of its piquancy, misnamed pepper (after the black peppercorn of the East Indies) by the Spanish explorers. This practice of mislabeling things because they are "like" other things has been going on for centuries and is something that musicians, particularly, have come to know and abhor. The labelers have given us such gems as "country rock," "jazz fusion" (melted jazz?), "Dylanesque," "adult contemporary," "pop rock," "dance music," "punk," "post punk," and my latest favorite, "New Age" music. Who does this stuff? I don't know, but then I don't know who names streets either. At any rate, there are roughly 200 different types of chilis in the world and nobody knows the names of all of them. So when we refer to a dish as "chili," what we really mean is chili (or chile) con carne—chili peppers with meat. Somewhere along the line, the *con carne* was dropped, additional spices were added, and the chili we know today evolved. Unfortunately, this evolutionary process also produced several aberrations that cannot be called anything but hogslop. In fact, let's get one thing straight right now: True, authentic chili does not—I repeat, NOT—have beans in it. Beans are a separate dish to be relished and revered in their own right. When you put beans in chili, you insult both the beans and the chili. Now, let's get on with it. Here's what you need to make real chili:

174

Texas Chili

INGREDIENTS:

A case of beer (preferably Mexican beer, but American
   or a light German beer will do). I prefer Corona,
   Bohemia, or Superior.

4 lb lean beef (I like to use a combination of 2 lb
   coarsely ground and 2 lb cubed)

3 medium onions, chopped

3 or 4 Tb vegetable oil or olive oil

2 8-oz or 1 15-oz can tomato sauce (not tomato
   paste). Whole or chopped tomatoes will do if you
   can't find tomato sauce

4 tsp salt

2 heaping tsp comino, also known as cumin, seeds or
   powder (it is best to grind seeds with a mortar
   and pestle)

6 or 8 cloves of fresh garlic, smashed or chopped

3 heaping Tb chili powder. If you live in Europe,
   call Gebhardt Mexican Foods Co. in San Antonio at
   (512) 227-0157 or the Pecos River Spice Co., P.O.
   Box 1600, Corrales, New Mexico (they have a phone
   number in New York for your convenience: (212)
   628-5374), and tell them you need some chili
   powder. If that fails, go to a Spanish market and
   see if you can buy some dried, red Ancho or
   Anaheim chili peppers. Take the seeds out (please
   take the seeds out-and don't rub your eyes). Then,
   grind, crush, chop, or otherwise mutilate these
   peppers as best you can.   continued

2 level tsp paprika

2 level tsp cayenne pepper

2 fresh jalapeño peppers (remove seeds and chop-
   do not rub eyes)

4 level tsp oregano

1 level tsp ground coriander or 2 tsp chopped
   fresh cilantro (same thing)

1/2 tsp ground black pepper

1 tsp Tabasco sauce

2 or 3 heaping Tb masa (corn) flour. If you can't get
   corn flour, regular wheat flour or ground yellow
   cornmeal will do.

Now, have a beer. If you have managed to round up all
of the above ingredients, you deserve one. It will
also help to give you the correct attitude for making
chili. In a large skillet, sauté the meat, onions,
and half the garlic in the oil until the meat is
grey. Then dump the meat, onions, and garlic into a
large pot with the tomato sauce. Rinse the tomato
sauce cans with beer and pour it into the pot. Get
yourself another beer. Spread the meat evenly over
the bottom of the pot. Add enough water so that the
meat is covered by 1/2". Add the remaining ingredients except the flour. (Note: The cayenne pepper is
what more or less determines the spiciness of the
chili. If you want hotter chili, use more. If you
want milder chili, use less). Heat all ingredients to
a mild boil, turn the flame down immediately, and
simmer for at least one hour and 15 minutes, stirring
occasionally to prevent sticking. Skim off excess
grease as it rises to the top. Mix the flour with
warm water to make a paste that is thick but
pourable. Add this to the pot while stirring and
simmer for another 30 minutes-or another 3 hours-it
just gets better. Have another beer.

Consider the above list of ingredients again.
Think about what a pain in the ass it is to
assemble them. Go to the phone and call Caliente
Chili, Inc., P.O. Drawer 5340, Austin, Texas
78763. Phone (512) 472-6996 and tell Gordon
Fowler or any of the other nice folks down there
that you are in dire need of some Wick Fowler's
2-Alarm Chili fixin's (that's "ingredients" to
you). They will send you as many packets as you
like of authentic, all natural, premeasured
ingredients to which you only have to add the
meat and the tomato sauce (I like to throw in
fresh onion and garlic, plus a little beer).
This will enable you to make a pot of chili
every bit as good (if not better) than the above
recipe with a helluva lot less trouble. And, no,
I don't own part of the company, I just like the
product. It's good stuff. Have another beer.

Somewhere in the West, Don Henley

Backyard Bar-B-Q!

INGREDIENTS:

Ribs, chickens, hamburgers, steaks, fishes,
   bacon-wrapped shrimps, and bologna (any one or
   combinations)

Potato salad

Baked beans

Corn on the cob

3-bean or combination salad

Potato chips

Fritos

Dip

Pickles

Olives

Carrot sticks

Celery stalks

Bar-b-que sauce (bottled or homemade)

Watermelon for dessert

Light the fire and cook all meats until tender and
   juicy. Hickory chips or mesquite as desired.

Serve everything buffet style and let the people
help themselves-everything's an appetizer. In
the event of rain, if you're in Memphis, go to
the Rendezvous; in Tulsa, go to Jamil's Steak
House; in Los Angeles, go to Dr. Hogly Wogly's
Tyler Texas Style Bar-B-Q. Anywhere else, you're
on your own. Good luck!!!

Jimmy Karstein, a.k.a. Global Village Hansen

Murphy's Corned Beef and Cabbage Stew

INGREDIENTS:
4 lb precooked Vienna corned beef
Garlic oil
1 red potato
1 white onion
1 carrot per person
1 container Spice Islands Pickling Spices
1/4 slice cabbage per person
1 loaf rye bread
Assorted mustards and pickles
3 cloves garlic, mashed
3 bay leaves
3 red chili peppers

Braise the beef in hot oil with the garlic oil of
your choice on both sides. Leave oil in pan. Place
all beef in pan. Add spices and fill 4/5 full of
water. Let cook (the water should slowly bubble) for
minimum of 6 hours. Replace water as it evaporates.
Add onion, potatoes, carrots 1 hour before serving.
Steam cabbage separately as you would any vegetables.
Drain the juice and use for gravy. Serve on platter.

This is a hearty meal that blues band leaders
like to eat right after they punch out the
drummer. The next day, the sandwiches are even
better.

Murphy Dunn

Quick Dinner

INGREDIENTS:
Thin cut T-bone steak
Vegetable oil
Fresh broccoli (small bunch)
Ear of corn still in shuck
Salt and pepper
Butter

Pan fry steak in vegetable oil. Steam broccoli.
Microwave corn 4 minutes with corn still in the
shuck (microwave 2 minutes, then turn).

For vegetarians, omit steak. If rushed for time,
omit broccoli. Be sure to microwave corn while
still in the shuck. Dinner in 4 minutes.

J. J. Cale

Biscuits and Gravy,
Country Style

INGREDIENTS:
1/2 lb bacon
4 cups self-rising flour
Crisco or lard
Buttermilk
Milk
Salt and pepper

Preheat oven to 450°. Fry 1/2 lb bacon. Remove bacon and use grease for gravy. Take 4 cups flour, mix in shortening or lard (2 large spoonfuls). Mix with hands until it feels grainy, then pour in buttermilk until doughy. Sprinkle some flour on mixing board. Roll out dough to 1" thick. Cut out biscuit. Place on well-greased baking pan or sheet. Put in oven for 10-15 minutes. Gravy: Put flour in bacon grease (enough to make a paste). Salt and pepper. Brown well. Pour in milk. Slowly cook until thick.

Bobby Bare

Fettuccine

INGREDIENTS:
1 package fettuccine noodles
1 1/4 lb butter
1 1/2 pints whipping cream
4 oz Parmesan cheese

Pepper

Blend butter, cheese, and cream in Cuisinart or high-speed blender. Cook noodles 7-9 minutes. Dry in colander. Pour sauce into emptied hot pot. Put noodles back into pot and toss. Add pepper to taste. Serves 3 or 4.

Tom Dowd

Delaney's Stew

INGREDIENTS:

2 1-qt cans of whole tomatoes with juice

2 cans English peas (drained)

5 whole cloves garlic, crushed

4 medium purple onions, chopped

Pinch of oregano

Double pinches of rosemary and thyme

1/3 cup cilantro

2 cups white wine

1 can beer

25 pods okra cut into quarters

2 15-oz cans new potatoes

2 cans button mushrooms

Olive oil

4 sliced boneless skinless chicken breasts

2 lb jumbo shrimp

Salt and pepper

4 broiled crab legs (optional)

Empty tomatoes and juice into a large pot. Add peas, garlic, onions, oregano, rosemary, thyme, cilantro, wine, beer, okra, potatoes, and mushrooms. Cook on low heat for 4 hours.

Coat a black iron skillet with olive oil and sauté chicken breasts, then add to pot. Sauté shrimp and add to pot. Add salt and pepper to taste. Cook on low heat for 2 hours. Serve with crab legs if desired.

Delaney Bramlett

Blackeyed Peas

INGREDIENTS:
Blackeyed peas
Fat back meat
4 pods okra
Salt
Cornbread

Let beans soak a while, put in a pot with meat, okra, and just a little salt. Boil for about an hour. Eat with cornbread made from Aunt Jemima's self-rising cornmeal.

Willie Nix
(Willie Nix is an Old Delta Bluesman who was the first artist to record for Sun Records.)

184

Frank Frost's Poke Sallet

INGREDIENTS:
Poke sallet
Salt pork
3 eggs

Pick a mess (2 grocery bags full) of young, medium-leaf poke sallet. Pick leaves from vein. Wash well. Boil for 10 minutes. Pour off black water. (It's poison.) Boil for another 10 minutes and pour off water again. Melt salt pork in black iron skillet while greens are cooking. Pour greens into skillet. Put 3 or more eggs into skillet. Stir egg into greens. Cook for about 30 minutes.

Frank Frost

Mississippi Mulligan Stew
(Hot & Spicy)

INGREDIENTS:
1 lb mixed beans (northern, pinto, large lima,
    kidney, green split pea, garbanzo, black bean,
    navy, etc.)
1 large onion, sliced
2 cloves garlic, minced
1 small can stewed tomatoes
2 bay leaves
1 tsp sugar
Dash of tabasco
1 tsp Worcestershire sauce
Dash of red pepper
1 lb smoked sausage or 1 lb smoked ham
Salt and pepper

Cover beans with water. Soak overnight. Next day,
wash beans thoroughly and drain. Add 2 qt water and
sausage or ham. Add tomatoes, onion, and all the
other seasonings. Bring to a boil and simmer 1 1/2 to
2 hours, until beans are tender. Add salt and pepper
to taste. Simmer 2 minutes.

Cajun seasoning can be used in place of the
other suggested seasonings; mixed beans are
available at most grocery stores and loose
beans may be found at most health food stores.

Fingers Taylor

Dan Penn's San Francisco Style
Bar-B-Q Chicken

INGREDIENTS:
Chicken breasts
Salt & pepper
Kraft regular Bar-B-Q sauce

Salt and pepper chicken breasts and bake them about
30 minutes at 350°-400° until they're about half
done. Have your grill ready. Put the chicken breasts
on the grill. Put sauce on the chicken when you first
put them on the grill. Cook them until they're black,
or even a little more. I like to tear 'em up a
little. Helps them get dry.

Dan Penn

186

A Fast, Low-Fat, Delicious (and Cheap) Chicken Dish

INGREDIENTS:
4 boned, skinless chicken breasts
1 small onion
1 small green bell pepper
1 15-oz can Hunt's diced tomatoes
1 15-oz can Hunt's tomato sauce
Some garlic powder and black pepper
    (but not too much!)

I guess you could use any part of the chicken in this dish but I like white meat and I have been on tour lately so I choose the breast. Carefully wash all chicken, because as we learned on <u>60 Minutes</u>, chickens have been known to bite the heads off pop stars while on stage, and are therefore unclean until rinsed. Then place them in a medium-sized baking dish and sprinkle them with garlic powder and black pepper. Not too much black pepper! Then cut up one small white onion and one small green bell pepper (yellow or red if you're on the charts this month) and put those around the chicken. Good. Now open one 15-oz can of Hunt's diced tomatoes (diced in sun-drenched tomato juice) and pour over the chicken. Then add a 15-oz can of regular Hunt's tomato sauce to that and you're ready to pop the whole thing into an oven preheated to 375° for 1 full hour. Serve over rice with steamed vegetables on the side, and you're about to experience some good, low-fat, delicious chicken eatin', and cheap! If you want to spice up this simple recipe a little, use a can of Rotel instead of (or in addition to) the tomato sauce! Bon Appetit!

Wayne Jackson, The Memphis Horns

Junior's Soul Slaw

INGREDIENTS:

1 medium head cabbage
1 red or white onion
2 celery
1 cup mayonnaise
1/2 cup sour cream
1/2 cup olive oil
1/2 cup prepared mustard
2 Tb vinegar
2 Tb honey
5-6 drops tabasco sauce
1 large carrot

Chop cabbage and mix ingredients together. Chill.

Jimmy "Junior" Markham

Wendy's Chicken

INGREDIENTS:
1 1/2 lb boneless chicken breasts
1 or 2 16-oz bottles thousand island salad dressing
1 envelope Lipton's onion soup mix
Peach preserves

Clean chicken and place in a baking dish with 1 3/4"
sides. Cover generously with onion soup mix. Cover
again with thousand island dressing until no chicken
shows. Dabble half-teaspoonfuls of peach preserves
over chicken (about 6 tsp altogether). Bake at 400°
for about 1 hour or until sauce is medium to dark
brown. Serve over long-grain and wild rice.

My son Clay and I think this is the best
chicken we've ever eaten. Clay would eat it
every night of the week if Wendy (my girlfriend)
would cook it.

Delbert McClinton

Linguine with Cream Sauce

INGREDIENTS:

2 Tb butter
2 Tb flour
Black pepper to taste
1 pint half & half
1 small carton sour cream
1/2 jar grated Romano cheese
1 Tb onion powder
1 Tb garlic powder
1 egg yolk
Linguine noodles for 4
1 Tb olive oil
1/2 tsp salt

In a saucepan, melt butter over medium heat and blend in flour. Add pepper. Pour in half & half. Stir until thick. Add sour cream and cheese. Continue stirring until well blended. Add the garlic and onion powder and stir again. Just before serving, blend in the egg yolk. Boil linguine in water with olive oil and salt.

This recipe was given to me by a Greek chef named Andy who at one time worked for Pete & Sam's restaurant in Memphis. For a heartier meal, I like to add sautéed shrimp and mushrooms with a little chopped green onion.

Steve Cropper

Texas Breakfast

INGREDIENTS:
Onions
Bell peppers
Canola oil
Corn tortillas
Eggs (1 or 2 per serving)
Salt & pepper
Cheese
Chili powder
Salsa
Flour tortillas or chips

Sauté diced onions and bell peppers in canola oil until tender. Cut corn tortillas in small pieces and add to onions and peppers. Mix until tortillas are soft. Push ingredients to the side of the pan and add beaten eggs (1 or 2 per serving). Scramble the eggs, adding salt, pepper, and grated cheese. When eggs are almost cooked, mix in the onions, peppers, and tortillas. Add a pinch of chili powder, mixing ingredients evenly in the pan. Then sprinkle more grated cheese on top and serve with salsa and soft flour tortillas or chips.

Gary Nicholson

Catfish Head Stew

INGREDIENTS:

Catfish heads

Onion

Garlic

Salt

Black pepper

A little red pepper

Oregano

Seafood seasoning

White potatoes (diced large)

Remove gills and eyes from fish head (throw away). Cover fish head with water in pot with seasoning. Cook for 20 minutes or so. Add potatoes. Cook until thick. Serve plain with crackers or over rice.

Little Milton

Rice 'n' Chicken

Boil the water for 5-10 minutes. Put the butter on top of rice. An' that is how I cook rice. I cook chicken with oil, salt, pepper, season salt, and hot sauce.

James "Son" Thomas

Bubble and Squeek

INGREDIENTS:
Sunday dinner leftovers
Boiled potatoes
Boiled cabbage (or any greens)
1 egg
Cooking fat (vegetable oil, butter, or lard)

Bung some fat in a frying pan: corn oil if you're a veggie, dead pig if you're not. Cut up the boiled potatoes and greens and bung 'em in. Fry high until crisp. Stir in the egg at halftime.

Bubble and squeek is a traditional English breakfast. I'm not sure but I believe the bubble to be the potatoes and the squeek to be the greens. Scrub bubble and squeek in equal proportions and add H.P. or Daddies' sauce to flavor. If not available, try Worcestershire or A1 steak sauce or anything.

Alvin Lee

Shepherd's Pie

INGREDIENTS:
6 large potatoes, peeled
1 cup milk
1/8 cup butter
1/8 lb cheese, grated
Lea & Perrins Worcestershire Sauce
6 OXO cubes (beef bouillon)
Salt and pepper
1 1/2 Tb cooking oil
3 lb ground beef (or turkey)
1 onion, chopped
2 cloves garlic, chopped
2 packages frozen mixed vegetables or 1 packet peas
3 carrots, diced
Any other leftovers from fridge
4 Tb flour
Mixed herbs, parsley, and Mrs. Dash

EQUIPMENT NEEDED:
4"-deep roaster pan (approximately 15" x 20")
Large frying pan
1 or 2 wooden spatulas or spoons and a muscular
    stirring arm

194

In the frying pan, preheat the cooking oil, add a little butter with seasoning and sauté the chopped-up onions and garlic. When you sense the right moment, tip in all the ground meat and stir vigorously. Pre-cook all your vegetables (peas should be mushy) beforehand so that when the meat is cooked medium rare, you can add them to your master mix. Pour in some of the vegetable water and add the flour. If the mixture gets too thick to manipulate, just add more hot water mixed with bouillon and all other seasonings you've been staring at. At this point, flavor-wise, you're on your own. Your assistant meanwhile should have boiled and mashed the potatoes. Add the milk and butter until they assume a creamy, smooth consistency. Place the piping hot cement into the roaster pan with leftovers, cover it all over with the mashed potatoes, and bake at 400° for about 20-25 minutes. Add the grated cheese and wait a couple more minutes until your pie is crowned with a lightly golden crust. And that's it.

It isn't necessary to have a fondness for sheep in order to appreciate the gourmet delight of a shepherd's pie. Despite its title, this meal contains no parts of God's woolly quadrupled nor of the shepherd himself. If you wish to know the true origins of its name, you'd better ask the cat because I sure don't know. All I can tell you is that it's an old English trick to get rid of leftover food and, once devoured, will weigh heavily in your stomach for days.

John Mayall

Chili Pie

INGREDIENTS:
3 cups corn chips
1/2 cup chopped onion
1 cup shredded cheddar cheese
1 can chili with beans
Sour cream and black olives (optional)

Layer 2 cups of corn chips, onion, half of the cheese, and chili in casserole dish. Top with remaining corn chips. Bake in 375° oven about 20 minutes. Top with remaining cheese and bake 5 minutes more. Garnish with sour cream and/or black olives (optional). Serves 3-4.

Sam the Sham

196

J. J.'s Famous Tuna Salad

INGREDIENTS:
1 7-oz can Bumblebee fancy albacore solid white tuna
   in soybean oil
2 grated hard-boiled eggs (boiled 12-15 minutes)
2 sweet baby gherkins chopped fine
1 Tb sweet pickle relish
1/3 Kraft salad dressing and 1/2 Kraft real
   mayonnaise (these are mixed to personal taste;
   Jimmy goes heavy on both)
3 scallions chopped, including green tops (optional)
5 chopped green olives, unstuffed (optional)
Kraft Sharp Cracker Barrel cheese

Drain tuna well. Shred until all is of same consistency (use fork-no food processor). Add all the
ingredients. Mix with fork by hand until consistency
is smooth and even. Use toasted whole wheat or Roman
Meal bread. Lightly coat each side of toast with
mayonnaise. Take cheese sliced thin (or grated) and
place on sandwich with tuna salad.

This tuna salad goes well on a bed of lettuce
with various crackers, cheeses (Brie is my
wife's favorite), and a light white table wine.

Jimmy Johnson
Muscle Shoals Sound

197

Smoked Venison

INGREDIENTS:
Deer ham
White bacon or beef tallow
1/2 tsp garlic salt
Black pepper
Everglades seasoning
Hickory (green if possible)
Buttermilk

Marinate deer ham 2 days in buttermilk. Plug ham with beef or bacon fat and seasonings. Cook slowly in cajun cooker with water between ham and heat. Do not cook well done; medium rare is ideal.

Richard "Dickey" Betts

198

Quiche

INGREDIENTS:
1 deep-dish 9" pie shell
1 cup whipping cream
2 eggs
1/4 chopped onion (optional)
6 oz ham
2 oz Swiss cheese
4 oz cheddar cheese
Salt and pepper

Layer the pie shell, first with shredded Swiss cheese, then onion, ham, and cheddar. Mix eggs and whipping cream until light and bubbly. Pour in pie. Bake at 350° for 50 minutes.

Bobby Manuel

Cranberry Casserole

INGREDIENTS:
3 cups apples, diced
2 cups fresh whole cranberries
1 1/2 cups sugar (1/2 brown)
1 stick margarine
1 1/2 cups uncooked oatmeal
1/2 cup brown sugar
1/3 cup flour
1/3-1/2 cup chopped pecans
1 tsp cinnamon

Layer apples, cranberries, and sugar in 2-qt dish.
To make topping, combine all other ingredients.
Spread mixture over cranberry and apples. Bake 75
minutes at 350°-375°. Great as a side dish to vegetables, but wonderful hot over vanilla ice cream!

John Kilzer

Barbecue Chicken

INGREDIENTS:
1 large bottle barbecue sauce
1 16-oz can Coca-Cola
1 fryer, cut up

Combine barbecue sauce and Coke in large saucepan and
bring to a boil. Add chicken and turn heat to low.
Cover and cook for 2 hours. May want to add more Coke
if needed. Take lid off and cook 20 minutes more.
Serve over rice.

Barry Beckett

200

Tuna Helper, Skillet Style

INGREDIENTS:
1 box Tuna Helper
3 Tb margarine or butter
1 cup milk
2 6-oz cans tuna

Stir together in 10" skillet: sauce mix, margarine or
butter, tuna (drained), milk, and 3 cups hot water.
Heat to boiling, stirring occasionally. Stir in uncooked pasta. Reduce heat, cover, and simmer 11 to 13
minutes, stirring occasionally, until pasta is tender. Remove from heat; uncover and let stand until
sauce is as thick as you'd like. 5 servings.

Eddie Hinton

Cornbread Dressing

INGREDIENTS:
1 batch cornbread
Neck, gizzard, and liver of chicken
1 1/2 cups water
3 cubes chicken bouillon
1 cup chopped onions
1 cup chopped celery
1/2 tsp poultry seasoning
1/2 tsp pepper
1 tsp salt
3 eggs, slightly beaten

Crumble cornbread into a large bowl. Stew together
the neck, gizzard, liver, salt, pepper, and chopped
vegetables in a stock made from the bouillon cubes
and water. Save pieces of the chicken for the gravy.
Add the remaining ingredients and mix thoroughly. If
necessary, use additional chicken stock. Cook for 20
minutes in a 2" deep greased pan at 450°.

Donnie Fritts

Band Meal

INGREDIENTS:
1-2 lb dry beans
Salt pork (small piece)
Onion
Green pepper
Green onion
5 lb potatoes
2 cans Rotel
Small bottle Wesson Oil
Molasses
Butter
1-2 boxes Jiffy Corn Muffin Mix
2 eggs
Milk (Small carton)

Check beans for rocks, etc. Rinse and cover with 2"
water. Soak overnight, or boil 2 minutes and let
stand with lid on for 1 hour. Drain and rinse. Add
Rotel and salt pork and fill (cover) with 2" water.
Bring to boil, then cover and reduce heat to simmer
until tender (several hours). Sauté onion and green
pepper in butter and add to beans just before serving. Slice and fry lots of potatoes in oil. Cook
cornbread according to directions. Serve beans with
fried potatoes, cornbread, molasses, and green onion.

Chuck Blackwell

Shirley's Chicken
Potato-Top Pie

INGREDIENTS:
1/2 cup chopped onion
6 Tb butter
1/2 cup flour
2 cups cooked, chopped chicken
10 oz frozen peas and carrots, cooled
3 cups chicken broth
4 oz pimento
Mashed potatoes

Sauté onion in butter until tender. Add flour and
cook for one minute. Stir in chicken broth and heat
until bubbly. Add chicken, peas and carrots, and
pimento. Pour into a casserole dish and top with
potatoes. Heat at 350° for 20 minutes. Serves 4.

Billy Crain

203

Squash Casserole

INGREDIENTS:
2-3 lb squash
1 onion, chopped
1 cup bread crumbs
1 cup shredded mozzarella cheese
1 cup shredded cheddar cheese
2 eggs (added when squash is cool)
1/2 cup parsley flakes
1/2 tsp salt
1/2 tsp pepper or to taste
Butter

Slice squash. Cover with water in a large pot and simmer until tender (about 20 minutes). Drain and mash. Add chopped onion, 1/2 cup bread crumbs, mozzarella cheese, cheddar cheese, eggs, 1/2 cup dried parsley flakes, salt, and pepper. Combine all ingredients until thoroughly mixed. Pour into large enough baking dish (greased with Pam, etc.). Top with additional cheese and bread crumbs, and drip melted butter over all. Cook uncovered in preheated oven at 350° for 45 minutes to 1 hour. Turn to broil for last 5 minutes to brown top.

Bruce Channel

Yankee Stuffed Chicken Breasts

INGREDIENTS:
12 boneless, skinless chicken breasts
12 slices stale bread
12 oz mild pork sausage
3/4 cup chopped celery
1/2 cup chopped onions
1 Tb corn oil
12 oz cream of celery soup
12 oz chicken broth
1 Tb chopped dried parsley
1 Tb rubbed sage
1 tsp dried rosemary
1/2 tsp thyme
1 can jellied cranberry

Contrary to popular southern belief, it is possible to make stuffing (dressing if you're southern) without cornbread. Begin by leaving 12 slices of sliced bread (loaf bread if you're southern) out overnight to allow bread to stale. Slice bread into 1/2" cubes and place in a mixing bowl. Crumble pork sausage into small pieces and sauté (fry if you're southern) until done. Drain grease (unless you have a death wish or redneck addiction to cholesterol) and add sausage to bread cubes. Sauté onion and celery in 1 Tb corn oil until soft and add to mixture. Add cream of celery soup, chicken broth, and spices to mixture and stir thoroughly. Let mixture sit (set if you're southern) while you pound chicken breasts with a wooden mallet to 1/4" thickness. Place 3 to 4 Tb mixture on each breast, roll breasts around mixture and secure with toothpicks. Bake in 360° oven for 50 minutes or grill over charcoal (barbecue if you're southern) until done. Slice cranberry into 1/4" thick rounds. Remove toothpicks from breasts and place on cranberry rounds. Serve with whipped potatoes (smashed taters if you're southern) and a fresh vegetable.

Terry Johnson

Brenda's Salsa Soup

INGREDIENTS:

6-8 homegrown tomatoes, peeled and chopped fine

6-8 spring onions (skinny scallions), chopped fine

2-3 Tb chopped cilantro

1 clove garlic, chopped fine

1/2 lemon, squeezed for juice

1 chili pepper, steamed until tender, seeds and veins
   removed, chopped fine

Sea salt to taste

Mix above ingredients in a large bowl. Serve at room
temperature in soup bowls. Crunch up and sprinkle on
top of each serving some white corn tostadas from 1
bag "restaurant style," lightly salted tortilla
chips. Serves 4.

I learned to make this in the summer of 1988 in
Gulf Shores, Alabama, from a natural medicine
woman down there named Brenda Sanchez. I was
suffering from a broken heart and this salsa
soup started me on the road to recovery! This is
best when prepared during the tomato season. The
fresher the tomatoes, the better the results. I
prefer homegrown Bradley tomatoes.

Marshall Chapman

Cilantro Pesto Pasta

INGREDIENTS:
2 garlic cloves
8 oz pesto
1 medium onion
1 bunch cilantro
1 medium tomato
2 Tb olive oil
1/2 cup nonfat milk
3 green chilies serranos
1/3 cup parmesan cheese
1 lb pasta

Cook pasta according to instructions. Mix all other
ingredients in a food processor. When pasta is ready,
drain and mix the sauce and pasta together.

*Note: Do not use all the sauce at once. Start with
1/2, then add the rest to your taste. Also, try
adding fresh mushrooms or sun-dried tomatoes.

Don Smith

Vegetable Casserole

INGREDIENTS:
1 can cream of mushroom soup
1 package shoepeg corn (Green Giant)
1 can drained French style green beans
1 cup chopped onions
1/2 cup sharp cheddar cheese, shredded
   (I prefer 1 cup)
1/2 cup chopped celery
1/2 cup sour cream
Salt and pepper
1/2 box cheese tidbit crackers
1/2 stick butter

Mix soup, vegetables, cheese, and sour cream. Add
salt and pepper to taste. Crumble cheese crackers,
mixed with butter, as topping for casserole. Bake at
350° for 45 minutes.

Jim Stewart

Jim Dickinson's Boiled Salad Dressing

INGREDIENTS:
1 Tb butter
1 cup apple cider vinegar and water (use just under 1
cup vinegar and add water to make 1 cup)
3/4 cup sugar
2 Tb flour
1/2 tsp salt
1 tsp dry or cream mustard
2 eggs
3/4 cup milk

Bring butter and vinegar and water to a boil. In a
bowl mix sugar, flour, salt, and mustard. Add eggs,
lightly beaten. Pour boiled vinegar into this mixture, beating with a wire whisk to take out lumps.
Pour into pan. Add milk. Cook, stirring constantly,
until thick.

Especially good mixed with grated cheddar cheese
and jars of pimentos to make homemade pimento cheese.

Jim Dickinson

Betty's Barbecued Shrimp

INGREDIENTS:

2 lb large shrimp, uncooked, unpeeled, heads removed,
   slit down the back
1/2 cup (1 stick) unsalted butter
3 Tb olive oil
3 Tb chili sauce
1 Tb Worcestershire sauce
1 Tb fresh lemon juice
1/2 lemon, sliced thinly
2 cloves garlic, minced
1 tsp minced fresh parsley
3/4 tsp ground red pepper
3/4 tsp liquid smoke
1/2 tsp paprika
1/2 tsp dried oregano
1/4 tsp hot pepper sauce
Salt and freshly ground pepper

Wash shrimp well, pat dry, and spread in shallow
baking pan. Combine remaining ingredients in small
saucepan and let simmer 10 minutes. Pour over shrimp
and mix thoroughly. Cover and refrigerate 2 or 3
hours, stirring every 30 minutes. Preheat oven to
300°. Bake shrimp covered about 15 or 20 minutes,
turning frequently, until they just turn pink. Do not
overbake. Serve in soup bowls with French bread to
soak up sauce. Just peel 'em, eat 'em, and enjoy!
Serves 4.

Bob Welch

Sid Selvidge's Jalapeño Cheese Grits

INGREDIENTS:
1 cup water
Pinch of salt
4 Tb grits
1/4" slice of jalapeño
Mexican cheese, cubed
Crumbled bacon

Add salt to water and bring to a boil. Add grits slowly and stir regularly to desired consistency. Right before serving, stir in jalapeño and cheese until melted. Top with butter and crumbled bacon.

Sid Selvidge

Billy Lee Riley's
Korn-Glamoration

INGREDIENTS:

2 15-oz cans whole kernel corn
4 1/2-oz can chopped green chilis
2 oz sliced pimentos
1/2 medium green bell pepper (diced)
2 cups cheddar and monterey jack cheese (mixed)
4 tsp cornstarch
1/2 tsp salt
1/4 cup evaporated milk
Juice from one of the cans of corn
2 Tb butter or margarine

Combine corn, chopped green chilis, pimentos, butter, evaporated milk, juice from corn, and salt. Place in 2-qt saucepan and bring to a boil. Mix cornstarch with enough water to dissolve, then add to above ingredients. Simmer until liquid is thickened. Remove from saucepan and place in 2-qt casserole dish in this manner: 1/2 of mixture in bottom of casserole dish, then a layer of cheese, then a layer of diced bell peppers. Put the rest of the corn mixture on top of the cheese and bell peppers, then put the rest of the cheese and bell peppers on top. Place in preheated 250° oven and bake for 45 minutes with cover. Serve garnished with thin slices of bell pepper.

I have been making this dish for the past 25 years. The way it came about, when I was living in Georgia back in the late '60s these ingredients were all that was left in my cupboard and so I just started mixing things together and this is what I came up with and it was a pretty good dish. Make some of it and let me know what you think about it. It's just a good ol' country dish.

Billy Lee Riley

Vegetable Senegalese Stew

INGREDIENTS:
2 large onions, finely chopped
4 Tb peanut oil
2 cups sweet potatoes, peeled and chunked
4 medium potatoes, peeled and quartered
2 large carrots, sliced
1/2 small cabbage, coarsely chopped
2 large tomatoes, quartered
1 package frozen spinach
1 tsp cayenne pepper
2 cups tomato sauce
3/4 cup peanut butter

Brown onions in peanut oil in a large stew pot. Add the vegetables one at a time, stirring after each addition. Stir in the tomato sauce and a cup of water. Add cayenne pepper. Simmer until all the vegetables are cooked, about 40 minutes. Scoop out a little hot broth and mix with the peanut butter, to make a more fluid paste. Add to the pot and cook for 15 minutes longer. Serve over rice. Enjoy! Serves 6.

John Hiatt

213

Lil's Cornbread

INGREDIENTS:

1 cup white, self-rising cornmeal, sifted
    (Sunflower white self-rising cornmeal is best!)
1/2 cup sifted self-rising flour
1 Tb bacon drippings (or Crisco) heated in iron skillet
1 egg
1 small glass buttermilk
1/2 tsp baking powder
1 Tb mayonnaise

Mix all together; should be like pancake batter or a little thicker. Heat an iron skillet, pour mixture in, and place in hot oven (500°) until browned nicely on top. Serve with hot butter.

Mike Duke

214

No-Cholesterol Corn Pudding

INGREDIENTS:

12 ears corn
2 cartons Egg Beaters (egg substitute)
3 Tb margarine
Skim milk
2 Tb flour
Nutmeg

Cut the kernels off the ears of corn and separate them with your fingers. Mix them into the two cartons of Egg Beaters. Melt 2 tablespoons of the margarine in a heavy saucepan, then stir in the flour. Beat in skim milk until you have a smooth, thin sauce. Blend this with the corn mixture and pour it into a 2-qt casserole that has been greased with margarine.

Set the casserole in an underpan of boiling water and bake in a 325° oven for about 1 1/2 hours or until a silver knife inserted in the center comes out more or less clean. Grate a dusting of nutmeg over the top of the pudding and dot the surface with bits of margarine. Return the casserole to the oven to bake for another 10 minutes. Serves 8.

Jerry Wexler, a record producer and connoisseur of good food who summers in East Hampton, was recently ordered to lower his cholesterol. With the help of his cook, Jerry worked out this delicious pudding, which is made with absolutely no butter, eggs, or cream.

Jerry Wexler

Easy Chicken Pot Pie

INGREDIENTS:
2 5-oz cans Swanson's premium chunk white chicken
2 15-oz cans Veg-all
10 3/4-oz cans creamy chicken mushroom soup
2 Pillsbury pie crusts

Place one pie crust in 9" x 9" pan or dish. Spread chicken in and cover with Veg-all. Mix 1/2 cup of water with soup and pour over Veg-all. Place top crust on and bake for 55 minutes at 350°.

Don Nix

216

Salmon Gravy

INGREDIENTS:
2 Tb cooking oil or drippings
2 Tb flour
1/4 tsp salt
1/8 tsp black pepper
6 oz milk or water
1 can drained salmon

On medium high heat, in a 10" skillet/pan, preferably cast iron, add cooking oil or drippings, flour, salt, and black pepper. Stir, allowing pasty mixture to brown. Pour in about 6 oz water, or substitute with 3 oz water, 3 oz milk. Stir, allow to heat to desired consistency. Add 1 can or less drained salmon. Heat 1 minute and serve with biscuits or bread. Is also good as a side dish or served over salmon croquettes.

Spooner Oldham

Webb Wilder's Jambalaya

INGREDIENTS:
4 chicken breasts
1 medium chopped onion
1/2 chopped green pepper
1 chopped celery stalk
1 whole fresh tomato
8 oz stewed tomatoes
1/2 tsp ground garlic
1/2 tsp salt
1/2 teaspoon pepper
1/4 teaspoon thyme
1/4 tsp red pepper
2 Tb Worcestershire sauce
1 package polish sausage
Parsley
2 Tb cooking oil
2 cups rice

In covered saucepan, cook chicken with water for
30-45 minutes. Remove chicken, cool, and cut into
bite-size pieces. Using oil, simmer onion, green
pepper, celery, tomatoes, and spices until done. Add
chicken. Brown sausage, and add to mixture. Add
Worcestershire sauce and parsley. Cook over low heat
for 2 hours. Serve over cooked rice.

Webb Wilder

Roger's Quick Cajun Fix

INGREDIENTS:
1 15-oz can Green Giant spicy chili beans
1 19-oz can Progresso lentil soup
2 cups cooked Minute brand instant whole grain rice
1 package Healthy Choice turkey sausage
1 Tb olive oil
3 Tb French's onion flakes
Tony Chachere's creole seasoning
Garlic powder
White pepper
Cayenne pepper
Salt
Tabasco sauce

Combine chili beans, lentil soup, onion flakes, and olive oil in saucepan. Stir and set heat to low. Make rice, following instructions on package. Stir in the cooked rice, cut 1 turkey sausage into round pieces (or you can use more), throw it in the pot, and stir. Now add Tony Chachere's creole seasoning to taste, set heat to medium low. Use the garlic powder, white pepper, cayenne pepper, salt, and tabasco sauce to your taste. This can get very hot! As soon as things start to simmer, it's ready!

Roger Hawkins

Brownies Coconutley

INGREDIENTS:
6 squares unsweetened chocolate
1/2 lb butter (unsalted)
2 cups sugar
4 eggs
2 Tb vanilla
1/2 cup all-purpose flour
1 tsp salt
1 cup chopped Macadamia nuts
1 cup semi-sweet chocolate mini morsels
1/2 cup shredded sweetened coconut, toasted in oven
Powdered sugar
1 trusty 8" x 8" brownie pan (greased)

Preheat oven to 325°. In a heavy saucepan, melt unsweetened chocolate and butter. Remove from heat. Stir in sugar. Beat in 4 eggs and vanilla. Quickly stir in flour and salt. Add nuts and chocolate morsels. Pour into trusty greased brownie pan. Bake 40 minutes. Remove from oven. Add toasted coconut and powdered sugar. Cool, then refrigerate. (These brownies are meant to be fudgy. Try to stay away from them until they are well cooled.)

Mike Utley

Upma, Also Known as
Swami Special

INGREDIENTS:

1 medium onion, peeled and sliced
1/2 cup broccoli or cauliflower, chopped
1/2 cup carrots, chopped
1 Tb cashew nuts, halved rectangularly
2 Tb almonds, blanched and halved
1 Tb raisins
2 cups farina or Cream of Wheat
2 Tb oil
2 Tb salt
1 Tb curry powder
2 Tb butter
1 Tb mustard seeds
4 cups hot water

In pot, heat oil until hot. Sauté salt, curry powder, and mustard seeds until they start to pop. Add onion and cook until it turns yellow. Add other vegetables, nuts, and raisins, and cook for 4 minutes over low flame. Turn up flame, pour in water, and bring to a boil. When boiling, pour in farina in a smooth, steady stream, stirring rapidly and constantly. (Be very careful when pouring the farina. Never dump all of it in or lumps will form. Stirring rapidly while you pour will make it smooth.) Be sure to turn down the flame when you do this so that the farina doesn't splatter on you. When mixture is firm, smooth over top and melt butter on it. A variation is to add Muenster cheese and apple slices to the top of the Upma. Bake at 250° until cheese melts and begins to brown.

This recipe was taught to us by our guru Swami Satchidananda, and has been enjoyed by our friends and family since the '60s.

Felix Cavaliere

Soba Noodles

INGREDIENTS:

1 package dried soba (buckwheat and mugwort combined)
1 bunch finely diced scallions-the green part is best
1 piece fresh ginger root
1 tin powdered wasabi
1/2 cup dry toasted sesame seeds
1 package dry fish flakes (bonita is best)
Low-sodium soy sauce (any brand)
Several toasted sheets of seaweed (if not available
    toasted, buy regular and toast it yourself;
    why not!?)

Boil noodles-al dente is best; can be eaten warm
or cool.

Broth or soup base: Boil fish flakes; drain and
add soy sauce to broth to taste (soy sauce is very
salty, so keep that in mind as you add it in; figure
approximately 1 cup broth per person). Put broth
mixture in refrigerator and chill. After sufficiently
chilled, add finely chopped scallions. Add fresh
ginger, grated to taste (ginger is pretty strong, so
keep that in mind as you add it-I happen to like lots
of ginger). Add wasabi paste (prepared according to
directions on tin) sparingly. You don't need much; it
is very strong and quite capable of clearing your
sinuses and bringing tears to your eyes. OK, the
broth is ready. Now, sprinkle the toasted sesame
seeds over the noodles and top it off with small,
fine, little strips of nori (seaweed) about 2" long.
The seeds and seaweed can actually be sprinkled over
the broth if preferred. I have found this dish (bowl,
actually) to be best served during the summer months-
very refreshing, light, and good carb energy.
Happy slurping!

Jim Keltner

Everybody's Favorite

INGREDIENTS:
Bologna (sliced thick)
Cheese (American, hoop, or head)
Crackers (Nabisco Saltines)
Red Nehi (large)

Willie Mitchell

Mama Valenzuela's Spanish Rice

INGREDIENTS:
Long-grain rice
1 onion
Olive oil
Fresh tomatoes or canned skinless tomatoes
Salt
Garlic salt
Pepper
Chicken broth

Cover the bottom of a sauté pan with olive oil. Then brown some long-grain rice. Don't be afraid to brown the rice a little longer than you normally would. Season with salt, pepper, and garlic salt. Toss in some diced onion to brown as well. Cut up some tomatoes and throw them in. Pour in 2 cups of chicken broth. Bring to a boil. Reduce heat to simmer; go ahead and season the whole mess again. Cover the pan and cook until rice is tender (25 minutes or so).

Jesse Valenzuela
Gin Blossoms

Meatless, Cheeseless Lasagna

INGREDIENTS:
6-8 lasagna noodles

TOFU FILLING:
2 Tb olive oil
2 cloves garlic, crushed
1/2 medium onion, chopped
1/2 tsp basil
1 Tb parsley
1/2 tsp oregano
2 cups crumbled tofu
2 eggs (optional)
1/4 tsp salt
1/4 tsp pepper

TOMATO SAUCE:
3 cups prepared spaghetti sauce
1 package pre-washed spinach
1/4 tsp salt
1/4 tsp pepper

PIMENTO SAUCE:
1 cup water
3/4 cup cashews
2 Tb sesame seeds
1 1/4 tsp salt
2 tsp onion powder
1/4 tsp garlic powder
1/2 cup pimentos

Cook noodles in salted water 15 minutes (this step is
optional). To make pimento sauce, combine sauce
ingredients in a blender (makes approximately 2 1/4
cups sauce). Set aside.   continued

In a large skillet put olive oil, chopped onion, crushed garlic, parsley, basil, and oregano. Cook until onion is tender. In a separate bowl, crumble tofu. Mix with eggs (if desired). Add onion mixture and mix well with 1/4 tsp salt and 1/4 tsp pepper. Pour spaghetti sauce in skillet and add spinach, turning slowly as it wilts. Season with salt and pepper.

In a 9" x 13" x 2" baking dish, put a <u>thin</u> layer of spinach/tomato sauce, then add the following in layers: 1/2 of the noodles, entire tofu/egg mixture, and 1/2 of the pimento sauce. Repeat with 1/2 the remaining spinach/tomato sauce, the rest of the noodles, the remainder of the spinach/tomato sauce, and the remaining pimento sauce. Bake at 350° for 45 minutes. Cool 10 minutes before slicing.

Danny Flowers